CROSSING
ROAD

Virginia Railroads

Volume 1:

Railroading in the Old Dominion

William E. Griffin, Jr. and Thomas W. Dixon, Jr.

Published 2010 by
TLC Publishing Inc.
18292 Forest Rd.
Forest, Virginia 24551
434-385-4076
www.tlcrailroadbooks.com

ISBN 9780939487974

Library of Congress Control Number 2010939581

Layout and Design by
Karen Parker

Printed in the U.S.A. by
Walsworth Publishing Company, Marceline, Mo.

Front End Sheets: Baltimore and Ohio Train No. 55, the "Valley Local", headed by Class B-18d Tenwheeler (4-6-0) No. 2028, makes a station stop at the Winchester station on October 26, 1946. (William E. Griffin, Jr. Collection)

Back End Sheets: Virginian motor No. 103 has a 73 car local freight crossing the New River into Virginia at Glen Lyn on September 4, 1953. (Richard Cook photo, TLC Collection)

Back Cover Top Left: Virginian Blue Ridge (2-6-6-6) No. 903 at Roanoke on August 31, 1957. The Virginian periodically moved these and other stored-servicable steam locomotives to keep the axle bearings properly lubricated, even after the retirement of all steam power. (Robert S. Crockett photo, William E. Griffin, Jr. Collection)

Back Cover Top Right: This painting by noted artist Andrew Harmantas depicts two RF&P "Governor" class 4-8-4s, Nos. 601 and 602, preparing to depart Richmond's Broad Street Station with passenger trains bound for Washington and the North, while a set of RF&P E8 diesels await their turn in the background. (TLC Collection)

Back Cover Center: SAL E units Nos. 3045 and 3020, along with Geeps Nos. 1965, 1962, and 1912, have a freight train in Richmond on September 7, 1957. (Ralph Coleman photo, William E. Griffin, Jr. Collection)

Back Cover Bottom: An N&W Y-6 2-8-8-2 on a coal train, with a bit of general freight on the head end, passing the Christianburg station on March 31, 1956. (William B. Gwaltney photo, William E. Griffin, Jr. Collection)

Table of Contents

This is the first in a series of books that we plan on the history and development of the railroads of Virginia. We are currently publishing a similar series on West Virginia, and plan to cover other states as well.

It is always somewhat of an artificial construct to consider railroads or a railroad within the political boundaries of just a single state, since railroads, by their nature, ignored political borders and stretched over areas that the market for their service and economic, geographical, and historical considerations and circumstances dictated. However, there is some rationale for considering the railroads operating in a particular region or state in that the railroads of that state were demonstrably key in its development.

The Commonwealth of Virginia, rich in history and cradle of much of American civilization, culture, and political thought, is an appropriate region in which to study the creation, development, and metamorphosis of railroading. The reader will note that the word "decline" is not used in the previous sentence. For those who have seen the railroads change from being the all-pervasive transportation system they were as late as 1950 into what they are today, are certainly convinced of their decline and fall. Indeed, there is much justification for this. However, even though railroads today are just one part of a huge transportation complex, their part is still a key element. As our society continues to evolve, the importance of railroad transportation also continues to evolve. Once assigned to the same trash bin of history as the horse and buggy, railroad technology is again becoming recognized for its efficiency, speed, ability to haul huge loads, fuel economy, ecological friendliness, and ability to move goods and people cheaply and efficiently.

The purpose of this book is to give the history of the railroads that served the Commonwealth of Virginia, whether they originated in the state, operated wholly within its bounds, or just entered it as part of a larger, far flung system.

Although it is the authors' intent to give an overview history of each line, the photos, maps, drawings, and data presented will concentrate on how the railroads of Virginia were constituted and operated in the mid-20th Century era of roughly 1935-1965. This is the era in which the transition of railroading occurred. At the beginning of this period railroads were the most important arteries transportation, but by its end they were being eclipsed by the newer forms of transport, especially highways and airlines, as well as inland waterways. It is also the era in which important elements of railroading reached their apogee of development. This included the passenger train, the steam locomotive, and the whole complex system of moving mail, package freight, express, and carload freight at a high degree of organization and efficiency. At the later part of the era it is also the era in which the passenger train and the mail and express it handled, was almost completely eliminated; and when less-than-car-load package freight was completely eliminated, supplanted by motor freight in highway trucks. With the decline in the common-carriage status of railroads at this time, their presence in the lives of ordinary citizens receded into a nostalgic miasma about the "good old days." And, of course, younger people did not have the railroad as a frame of reference of any type in their lives. It is the era in which the time-honored steam locomotive was completely replaced by the diesel-electric locomotive that we know today. During this time the town's station with its friendly agent was closed because he no longer needed to sell tickets to passengers or to handle freight for individuals and businesses. As a result, these and other facilities, needed for accommodating the business as it was then constituted, were closed, downsized, or removed, including stations, yards, shops, etc.

Therefore, this is an appropriate era in which to concentrate the contents on this book. Much of this era is still in living memory or not far removed. Much of it is firmly affixed in the collective memory and consciousness of our society, and it is a valuable period in which to sample in a small way the consequences of fairly drastic and reasonably fast change in transportation modes and systems.

One of the major markets for this book, we know, is a group of people who are hobbyists who model railroads and some who simply study them.

These are usually called "railroad scale modelers" and "railfans" respectively. There will be another audience, we hope, in people who are interested in the historical and economic development of Virginia and the part that railroads played in that.

Virginia is situated on the eastern seaboard of the United States, about halfway between the highly populated and traditionally industrialized Northeast and the traditionally rural, more sparsely populated, agrarian Southeastern region. It also serves as a gateway to the Midwestern region; therefore, geographically it was a crossroads region as railroads began to expand and build to meet existing needs or to open new territories and business.

With the huge ice-free harbor on Hampton Roads at the mouth of Chesapeake Bay, it was ideally situated for a good shipping trade both along the coast and to European and other foreign ports. In its western areas, coal exists in some quantity and has been extracted for transport both east and west, although its coal reserves are small in comparison with its sister state, West Virginia. Many of the coal haulers which extracted West Virginia and Kentucky coal, however, transported much of it through Virginia. The Commonwealth has good rivers and some of them could be exploited for transportation, most notably the James River, along which the James River & Kanawha Canal was built before the War Between the States.

Railroads began their development within Virginia early in the railway age because the region was already well developed with cities and towns, water transport, ocean shipping, and stable political institutions. At least this was true in the eastern portions of the state. Of course, the western regions, beyond the Alleghanies, eventually went their own way as the new state of West Virginia in 1863.

Once railway technology was created, it burst with great speed in America, so that within the space of just twenty years transportation by rail had begun to transform almost every aspect of life. This would only continue in the coming decades until a highly developed, standardized, interconnected system of railroads was operating in the early part of the 20th Century. Virginia befitted by its previously mentioned crossroads location and many large, important railroads operated within the Commonwealth. Most important of these, as they were known in the mid-20th Century, were:

- Southern Railway - This road operated its main line diagonally southeasterly-northwesterly across the state from Washington, D. C. to Danville, with other ancillary lines and branches serving specific areas of the state. It had a large system of lines in the Southeastern states.

- Norfolk & Western Railway - N&W ran almost east-west across the lower portion of the state, from Norfolk to Bluefield and Bristol. It had numerous lines in the southwestern portion which served the coal producing region. It also operated an important through freight and coal line up the Shenandoah Valley between Roanoke and Hagerstown, Maryland. Begun in Virginia, N&W had its corporate, main operating, and mechanical headquarters in Roanoke.

- Chesapeake & Ohio Railway - C&O's line likewise ran roughly east-west through Virginia, with some branches serving particular regions. Between Clifton Forge and Richmond it had two mainlines, one via Charlottesville and Staunton, and the other down the James River through Lynchburg. It used these lines mainly for coal transport to Newport News. The C&O was native to Virginia and had its main corporate headquarters in Richmond during much of its life.

- Virginian Railway - The Virginian was a late-comer to railroading. Completed in 1909, it was built strictly to transport West Virginia coal to Norfolk for water shipment. Its effect on the state's development was probably the least of the major railroads in Virginia. Another railroad native to Virginia, the Virginian had its major headquarters in Norfolk.

- Atlantic Coast Line Railroad - This road had only a short portion of its main line in Virginia, between Trego, on the boarder south of Petersburg, and Richmond. The bulk of its system was to the south. However it was forced to deliver all its through business at Richmond to be forwarded to and from the northeast.

- Seaboard Air Line Railway - Similar in nature to the ACL, it ran only a short distance between the North Carolina border and Richmond. In the mid-20th Century era of this book, both it and ACL had a very large through passenger train operation between the northeast and Florida. SAL had it corporate headquarters in Portsmouth, and later in Richmond for the bulk of its life.

- Richmond, Fredericksburg & Potomac Railroad - This short 113-mile straight north-south line ran between Richmond and Washington and served as a funnel through which all the business between the northeast and the deep south was routed. Though a short line, it was one of the busiest in the state. All through business over the ACL and SAL flowed over the RF&P. RF&P was headquartered in Richmond.

- Baltimore & Ohio Railroad - This important Northeastern/Midwestern line, which was America's first commercial railroad, had a limited presence in Virginia, with only one line running down the Shenandoah Valley as far as Lexington. It had little business and was largely abandoned by the era of this book.

- Atlantic & Danville Railroad - Operated between Norfolk and Danville in what is termed "Southside Virginia" just north of the North Carolina border, this line was little more than a short-line railroad that catered to regional needs.

- Besides these lines, the Louisville & Nashville just touched the state for a few miles in the far southwestern portion's coal regions. The Clinchfield Railroad had an important portion of its coal producing area as its main line passed north-south through the far southwestern portion of the state. The Pennsylvania Railroad, giant of the Northeast, had a few miles of line that operated into RF&P's large Potomac Yard in Alexandria, just to the south of Washington, and owned a line running down the Delmarva Peninsula ("Eastern Shore") of Virginia terminating at Cape Charles, where ferry operations brought its traffic to Norfolk.

- The other railroads in Virginia were in the short-line or logging railroad, and several of thise are treated in short chapters at the end of the book. These and others will be covered in more detail in a future volume.

It is hoped that this overview book will give the reader a flavor of railroading in Virginia in the mid-20th Century and a nostalgic yet accurate and informative look back at the railroads of the Commonwealth when they were at their height of importance and visibility.

William E. Griffin, Jr.

Thomas W. Dixon, Jr.

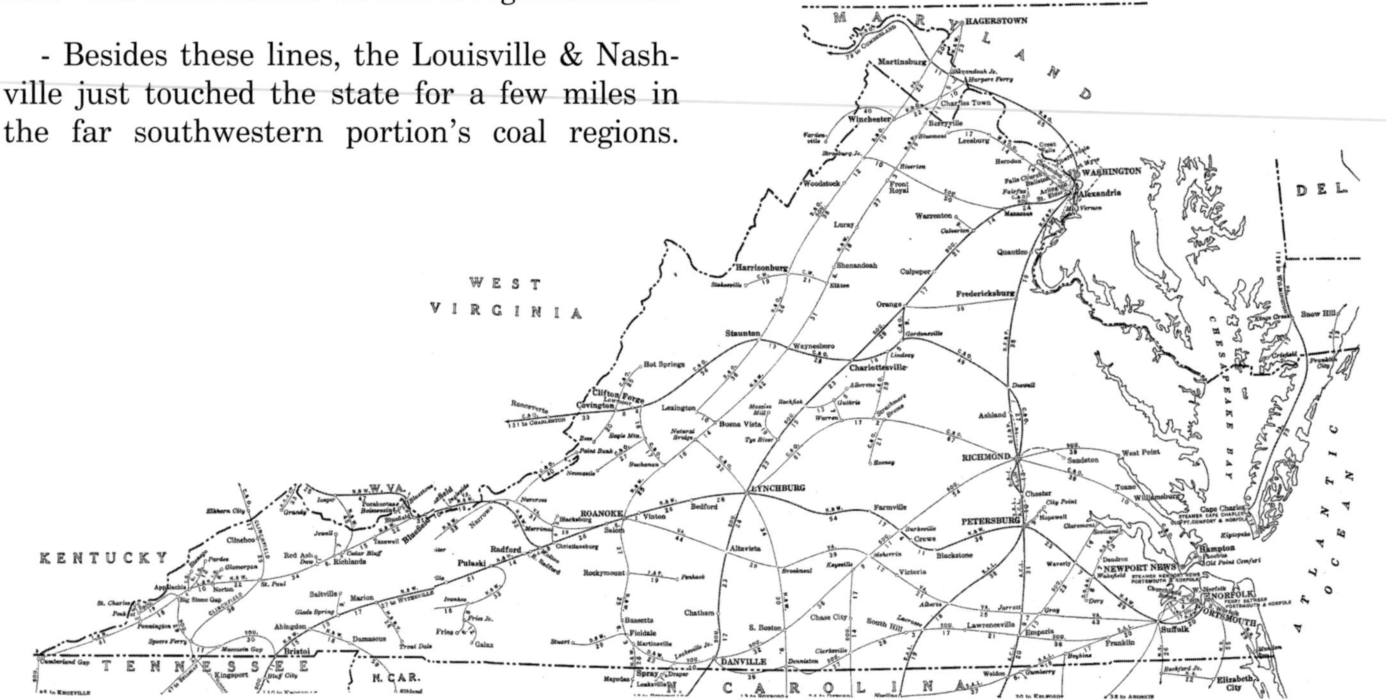

The Chesapeake & Ohio's earliest predecessor line was the Louisa Railroad. In 1837 it built its line from the central Virginia county of Louisa to a junction with the Richmond, Fredericksburg & Potomac Railroad at what is now Doswell to help farmers get their products to market in Richmond. The line was leased to the RF&P until 1847 when the owners began independent operations. By 1851 it was extended into Richmond (over the objections of the RF&P), and in the west reached Gordonsville and Charlottesville. In line with the new ambitions of the road it was renamed Virginia Central in 1850, with a charter to build to Covington, at the foot of the Allgehanies, where connection would be made with a state-sponsored Covington & Ohio Railroad, leading to the Ohio River.

Between 1850 and 1857 the Virginia Central was built across the Blue Ridge through the help of the state-sponsored Blue Ridge Railroad, then across the Shenandoah Valley and North Mountain to Jackson's River Station (now Clifton Forge) about nine miles short of Covington. Here construction stopped when the War Between the States intervened.

The Virginia Central was a very important Confederate line during the war, carrying huge amounts of supplies and troops. It was also used in tactical operations. By the end of the war the railroad was badly damaged, yet by late 1865 was back in operation. The owners wanted to extend westward and in 1869 got Collis P. Huntington to back the venture. He was fresh from completing the Central Pacific portion of the Transcontinental Railroad and had the idea that he wanted to create a true transcontinental system under one person's control–his.

With Huntington's backing, the line, now renamed Chesapeake & Ohio, built across the wilds of the southern part of the new state of West Virginia, reaching the Ohio, and the new line was opened in May, 1873. Huntington's aim was to make C&O the eastern connection of his system of railroads from the west.

Initial traffic on the C&O was mainly local and consisted largely of mineral, forest, and farm products. It was not until the 1880s that coal traffic became important. It was coal that would make the C&O, and with each year that traffic grew.

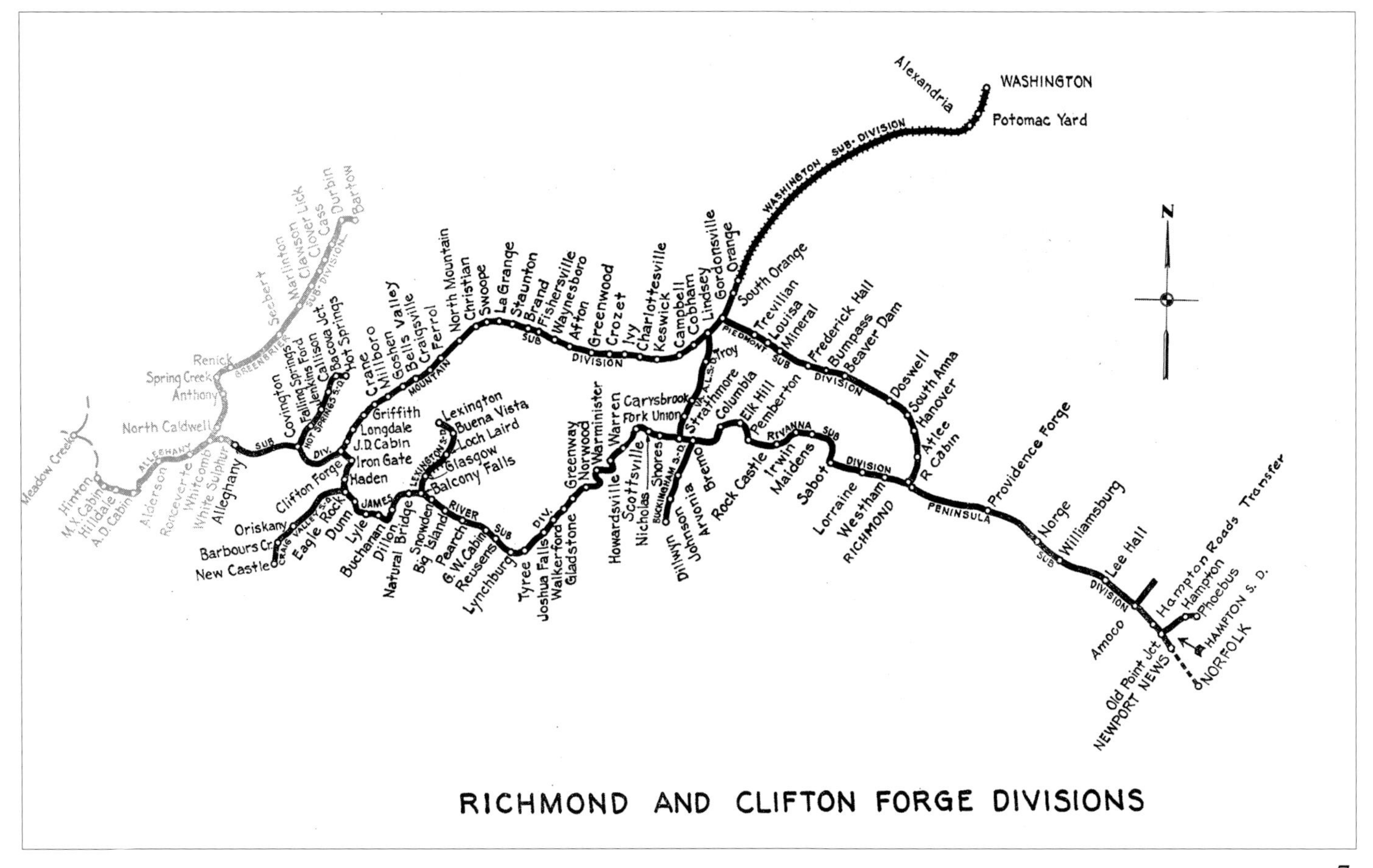

In 1881 C&O built a line down the Peninsula from Richmond to Newport News, opposite Norfolk on the great Hampton Roads harbor. Here it provided a pier to transfer coal to ships and barges bound for the northeastern U. S. and overseas. The eastbound coal traffic to Newport News would be the largest portion of C&O's business until about 1915, when coal traffic moving to the industrializing Midwest began to equal or exceeded it in volume.

In the era before railroads George Washington himself became president of the James River & Kanawha Canal with the aim of connecting Tidewater navigation with the Ohio-Mississippi system. This canal was built as far as Buchanan, Virginia, by 1860, but after the war railroad technology was proving so much better than canals that the canal fell into disfavor. The Richmond & Alleghany Railroad bought the canal and built a line from Richmond through Lynchburg to Clifton Forge along the tow-path of the canal. The R&A was bought by C&O in 1890 and from that day until the present has provided it an excellent route for eastbound coal, avoiding the heavy mountain grades of the old Virginia Central line via Staunton and Charlottesville. Because C&O bought the R&A, which was successor to the Canal, the C&O advertising men of the 1930s began calling the C&O "George Washington's Railroad," since he was president of a predecessor company.

By 1881 C&O had acquired Huntington's planned western connection over roads he owned via Louisville and Memphis to New Orleans, and for a brief period 1888-89 he controlled a true transcontinental, but it couldn't be held together and the C&O portion went into Vanderbilt and Morgan hands.

By the 1890s C&O's coal business was growing so rapidly that the line had to be completely rebuilt, which occurred under the new owners. They installed M. E. Ingalls, who was president of the New York Central-controlled Big Four Railroad (Cleveland, Cincinnati, Chicago & St. Louis). With the new backing the C&O was rebuilt, refurbished, and upgraded to better accommodate the booming coal traffic.

In 1889 the new owners negotiated for trackage rights over the Virginia Midland Railroad (Later Southern Railway) from Orange to Washington, thus giving access to the Northeastern railroad network. In that year C&O began its high-profile named-train passenger service from New York (via the Pennsylvania Railroad connection), and Washington to Cincinnati, where connections were made via the Big Four to Chicago, Indianapolis, and St. Louis. Though passenger business remained a tiny fraction of C&O income, it would lavish a great deal of money, advertising, and interest in the service in the following sixty years. In 1888 C&O completed a line along

A car float is seen here arriving at Newport News from Norfolk in 1945 with a load of box cars. The car floats had a small engine for maneuvering and steering, but had to be pushed or pulled across the harbor by tugs. The C&O yard at Brooke Avenue in Norfolk was completely isolated and could be reached only by water. C&O shared its Norfolk facility with the Pennsylvania Railroad, whose ferries from Cape Charles used the station and pier there. (C&O Ry. Photo, C&O Hist. Soc. Coll., CSPR-57.147)

the south (Kentucky) side of the Ohio River and across that stream into Cincinnati. The first through train over the new C&O routing was the *Fast Flying Virginian* inaugurated May 11, 1889. Of course, C&O still continued to operate passenger trains between Newport News and Charlottesville, where they were consolidated with trains from Washington. C&O also established a small yard in Norfolk and began serving that city by car float, barge, and passenger ferry from its terminals at Newport News.

This 1957 photo shows numerous colliers waiting in the stream as three ships are loaded at C&O's two Newport News coal piers in 1957, during a big export coal boom. (C&O Ry. Photo, C&O Hist. Soc. Coll., CSPR-3841)

In the years from 1890 to 1915 scores of branch lines were built in West Virginia and eastern Kentucky, which tapped some of the richest coal deposits in the east, and the coal business ballooned. As explained before, eastbound traffic to Newport News through Virginia, accounted for a large part of this until about 1915, when as much began to move west as east. However, both sides of the traffic continued to expand.

In 1910 the Hocking Valley Railway of Ohio was acquired, which gave C&O an outlet for its coal to the Great Lakes at Toledo. It leased trackage rights on the Louisville & Nashville to Louisville, and thus the modern C&O system was in place.

In Virginia, in 1889-90, Clifton Forge was built as a major shop area and terminal and became the eastern hub of the system, while Huntington, W. Va., and Russell, Kentucky, became the western hubs. Three major mainline subdivisions radiated from Clifton Forge. First, the old Virginia Central line, called the Mountain Subdivision,

An aerial view shows part of the large coal-storage yards at Newport News and the two coal piers (upper center). Out of the photo to the bottom are the merchandise, ore, and passenger piers. To the west an even larger yard was used for storage before the cars were brought to this point for dumping. (C&O Ry. Photo, C&O Hist. Soc. Coll., CSPR-3578)

A war-time crowd of passengers is boarding the westbound Sportsman *at the Newport News passenger station and pier. Passengers transferred to and from trains and ferries at this covered pier. (C&O Ry. Photo, C&O Hist. Soc. Coll., CSPR-124)*

ran to Staunton, Waynesboro, and Charlottesville, where it forked again, the Piedmont Subdivision running down to Richmond and the Washington Subdivision operating to Orange and over the Southern Railway into Washington.

Second, the James River line ran along that river through Lynchburg to Richmond. Third, the Alleghany Subdivision ran westward from Clifton Forge, across Alleghany Mountain (in this part of Virginia Alleghany is spelled with an "a") and terminated at Hinton, West Virginia

The Mountain Subdivision handled all the through passenger trains as well as fast freight headed for the Northeastern connections. The James River Line handled the eastbound coal but had only local passenger business, as well as some fast freight headed to and from the ocean terminal. The Alleghany, of course, handled all the coal, freight and passenger business to and from the west, leaving Virginia at the crest of Alleghany Mountain.

The shops at Clifton Forge handled all steam locomotive repair for the eastern end of the road, and always remained the second most important mechanical repair facility on the C&O.

At Richmond the Piedmont Subdivision entered from the northwest, and the James River Line (Rivanna Subdivision) from the west. In 1901 a major rebuilding of terminals at Richmond resulted in the construction of the mile-and-a-half James River Viaduct, which carried C&O coal trains from the Rivanna Subdivision, avoiding the congestion of the city, to a new facility at Fulton yard, on the city's eastern edge.

As a part of this work a large new station was built on Main Street, which accommodated C&O and Seaboard Air Line Railway passenger trains. It still stands today, largely preserved and now again host to Amtrak passenger trains operating on the old C&O line to Newport News.

Eastward from Richmond the Peninsula Subdivision ran about 85 miles to Newport News on a fairly straight alignment with good grades.

From the old Richmond & Alleghany along the James River, C&O inherited some branch lines. The Buckingham Branch ran from Bremo, about 66 miles west of Richmond, for about 17 miles to Dillwyn, handling local agricultural and forest products, as well as soapstone and other mineral products. In the 1980s it was abandoned and was bought by the Buckingham Branch Railroad and today operates very successfully as a short line. The Buckingham branch mainline terminal was at Strathmore, just a mile and a half west of its connection with the Rivanna Subdivision at Sabot. Strathmore was also the terminal for the Virginia Air Line Subdivision. This short line was built as an independent railroad in 1909 and ran from this point to the C&O Washington Subdivision at Lindsay, Va., It was bought by C&O in 1912, and was maintained mainly as a secondary by-pass route since it originated little traffic. It was used for coal headed to Washington and points east, thus bypassing the mountain grades.

From Warren, about 85 miles west of Richmond, the Alberene branch tapped soapstone deposits to the north of the C&O and was a marginal operation, lasting to the 1960s.

The Lexington Branch ran from Balcony Falls (Glasgow) to Lexington, and was mainly for local business. In 1905 the line was consolidated with Norfolk & Western's Shenandoah Valley line from a point near Balcony Falls to Buena Vista. The branch operated until it was washed out by a Hurricane-induced flood in the 1970s.

At Eagle Rock, about 17 miles east of Clifton Forge, the Craig Valley Branch extended 26 miles to New Castle, Virginia. It was built to carry iron ore in the era when Virginia was an important iron producer, but the deposits were not as rich as expected and the line continued its life as a local carrier occupied with a marginal traffic in agricultural and forest products. It was abandoned in 1961 and much of its right of way became a state highway.

On the Alleghany Subdivision, the Hot Springs branch ran northward from Covington 25 miles to Hot Springs. It was built in 1890 to provide passenger service to and from the new Homestead Resort Hotel at that point. The hotel was purchased by C&O president Ingalls, and developed into one of the east's premier mountain resorts, which it remains today. The branch was mainly for passenger business, transporting through sleeping cars. These cars arrived at Clifton Forge, mainly from New York City, and there dropped there by the name trains. They were made up in to trains that took them up the branch to Hot Springs at convenient times and returned them to the mainline to be attached to trains operating back to Washington and New York. In was abandoned in 1970, spent a few years as a tourist line, and was then taken up.

The other branch from Covington was the Potts Creek Subdivision, which was another line built for iron ore extraction. Again, the expectations were false and no appreciable traffic developed. The line was built 1906-1908 and was abandoned in 1934.

Two short branch lines for Sulphur Mines and other mineral production extended from Mineral, on the Piedmont Subdivision, but were abandoned before the era of this book's emphasis.

Passenger operations were centered in Charlottesville, where the mainline name trains were broken up and consolidated. Trains arriving from the west were broken with one section headed to Washington and the other to Newport News, and westbound trains from Washington and Newport News were consolidated here.

C&O's headquarters offices were, of course, in Virginia when its lines largely operated there, and after its expansion Richmond remained as its center of operational, mechanical, engineering, and administrative control. This changed in the period 1890-1900 when the Big Four controlled, with executive and many administrative offices in Cincinnati and Washington. After 1900 the headquarters returned to Richmond. From the 1930s onward the highest executive offices were in Cleveland, as a result of the Van Sweringen control. Mechanical and engineering offices left in the early 1960s to Huntington, W. Va., and many other offices were gradually consolidated and closed, a process that was completed during the C&O/B&O merger years. Successor CSX Corporation returned to Richmond in the 1980s, but then all its operations were eventually consolidated in Jacksonville, Florida, and the last vestiges of C&O's headquarters were gone from Richmond.

Some of C&O's huge 2-6-6-6 Allegheny type simple articulated locomotives were used on the Peninsula Subdivision, shuttling heavy coal trains and long empties the 85 miles between Richmond and Newport News. They were so heavy that they could only be brought across the James River Viaduct in Richmond with empty tenders and boilers. Once at Fulton they were captive to the Peninsula line. Here No. 1630 is eastbound with coal about ten miles east of Richmond on June 2, 1947. (J. I. Kelly Photo, D. Wallace Johnson Collection)

Another "big" locomotive used on the Peninsula during the later years of steam was the T-1 2-10-4 Texas type, which, like the H-8, was captive to the line because of its weight. Here one of these superb Super Power locomotives in headed east with coal past the ancient station at Providence Forge in July 1952. (J. I. Kelly Photo, C&O Hist. Soc. Coll., COHS-212)

Fulton was C&O's major yard in Richmond. Located on the eastern edge of the city, coal trains arrived here across the famous James River viaduct from the Rivanna Subdivision, and freight and passenger trains funneled here off the Piedmont Subdivision. The roundhouse and terminal area seen here in about 1958 show how the roundhouse was built at three different times to three slightly differing sizes and styles. (C&O Ry. Photo, C&O Hist. Soc. Coll., CSPR-3573)

Westbound out of Richmond on the Rivanna Subdivision, a C&O K-3a 2-8-2 Mikado takes an empty coal train along the old JR&K Canal (left) and the James River (right). It has some mixed freight tacked on the head-end as was often the case. (J. I. Kelly Photo, C&O Hist. Soc. Coll., COHS-313)

At Strathmore, K-2 No. 1200 is seen just east of the coaling station, while a G-7 2-8-0 rests at the terminal in the background in May 1951. Strathmore served as the terminal point for the Buckingham and Virginia Air Line (VAL) branches. The G-7 was for use on the Buckingham Branch. 2-8-2 Mikados of the K-2, K-3, and K-3a classes were standard power on the James River Line. (H. Reid Photo)

In this scene the Buckingham Branch local's G-7 2-8-0 is sandwiched in the middle of its train as it maneuvers after crossing the James River bridge (left). The old wooden combination car accommodated passengers on this slow mixed train. Note that there are hoppers and gondolas for mineral products at right, and in the rear empty bulkhead flat cars for pulp wood. The branch is operated today by the short line Buckingham Branch Railroad and is highly successful. (J. I. Kelly Photo, D. Wallace Johnson Collection)

The Alberene Branch ran from Warren to Esmont thence to Guthrie and Alberene, mainly to tap soapstone resources. It was abandoned from Guthrie to Alberene in 1936 and the balance to Warren in 1960s. It connected with the Nelson & Albemarle short line at Esmont. An N&A saddle-tank 2-4-2 is seen here at Schuyler in 1950. N&A trains operated over the Alberene branch as well, to Warren. (TLC Collection)

With a great show of exhaust G-7 Consolidation No. 893 has the Buckingham Branch train near Arvonia in May 1951. (H. Reid Photo, TLC Collection)

The Virginia Air Line Subdivision ran between C&O's Rivanna Subdivision at the Washington Subdivision and was used mainly for coal headed to Washington. This avoided the heavy mountain grades. Merchandise between Newport News terminal and Washington was also carried over this line. Here freight No. 404 is passing the neat station at Palmyra on September 26, 1951. (H. Reid photo, TLC Collection)

One of the typical Mikados, this time K-3a No. 2335, has a coal train at the west end of the passing track at Eagle Rock in June 1952, a typical C&O cantilever signal bridge to the right. The Mikados were adequate power for heavy coal trains since the James River ine was on a fairly steady descending grade. (Gene Huddleston Photo, C&O Hist. Soc. Coll., COHS-1044)

K-3 No. 1257 is seen here on May 10, 1951, in the small interchange yard at Balcony Falls (known on Virginia maps as Glasgow). At this point C&O interchanged traffic with N&W's Shenandoah Division, and also dispatched trains over the Lexington Branch. The branch line trains used N&W from here to Buena Visita before returning to C&O rails. (John Krause Photo, TLC Collection)

Passenger service on the James River line been Richmond and Clifton Forge consisted only of local accommodation trains, and after 1930 they were exclusively Brill Gas-Electric cars. Here No. 9053 has a trailing combine car in tow at Natural Bridge in October 1954. The last two trains were discontinued in 1957. (J. R. Kean Photo, C&O Hist. Soc. Coll., COHS-3376)

The Lexington Branch mixed train is seen here with wooden combine No. 418 leaving Lexington for Balcony Falls in the winter of 1949. C&O connected with B&O's Shenandoah Valley line until that road was abandoned south of Staunton, at which time C&O took over B&O's station in the town of Lexington and used it until the line was abandoned in the early 1970s. (J. R. Kean Photo, TLC Collection)

The Craig Valley Branch local is seen here toward the end of its days about 1957 with a new S-2 Alco switcher, a box car, three pulpwood loads, and a caboose. Three years later the branch was taken up and the right of way sold to the Commonwealth of Virginia, which built a road on it. The branch was built in 1889-91 and was intended to haul iron ore, but the deposits never panned out. (TLC Collection)

The Piedmont Subdivision, which was the original line of the old Louisa Railroad in the 1840s, was primarily a passenger railroad in the 20th Century, with a little merchandise freight thrown in. Here E-8 No. 4026 and a mate have the Virginia section of the George Washington *(Train No. 42) at Doswell. The station sits in the Wye here formed by C&O as it crossed the RF&P mainline (foreground). (S. K. Bolton Photo, TLC Collection)*

C&O's Washington Subdivision comprised mainly trackage rights over the Southern Railway's mainline between Orange and Alexandria, and was used by C&O's through name passenger trains and fast freights. Here Streamlined L-1 Hudson No. 492 is flashing through Cameron Run just south of Alexandria, with a long heavyweight train, probably the westbound George Washington, in about 1949, just before arrival of the new lightweight cars. At this point C&O trains transitioned from RF&P tracks to SR tracks for the run southwest to Orange, where C&O trackage was attained for the remainder of the trip into Charlottesville. (John Krause Photo, TLC Collection)

In this view C&O 2-10-2 No. 2854 is at milepost VM 8.5 on the Southern just south of Alexandria with an extra freight of largely empty hoppers on September 24, 1950. Coal bound for Washington and points north or east usually moved via the James River line to Strathmore, then over the VAL to Lindsay on the Washington Subdivision, and then on north. In this case the empties are probably returning via Charlottesville and the Mountain Subdivision. 2-10-2s, a very unusual type on C&O, were used on this line almost exclusively. (J. I. Kelly Photo, D. Wallace Johnson Collection)

Right: The Mountain Subdivision between Charlottesville and Clifton Forge was part of the old Virginia Central, built in the 1850s, and surmounted some of the steepest grades on the entire mainline, thus it was reserved mainly for passenger trains and fast freights headed to and from Washington. Here two J-3 class 4-8-4 Greenbrier types, led by No. 606, power a long heavyweight train near Little Rock Tunnel on the east slope of the Blue Ridge in July 1949. Two large locomotives (either 4-8-4s or 4-8-2s) were required on the Mountain if the train exceeded 14 cars. (J. I. Kelly Photo, C&O Hist. Soc. Coll., COHS-316)

Below: Blue Ridge Tunnel was built in 1854 and was one of the longest in the world at the time. C&O bored a new tunnel here in 1948. C&O J-3a class 4-8-4 Greenbrier type No. 614 exits the new tunnel westbound on July 15, 1938 with Train No. 47, The Sportsman. (J. I. Kelly Photo, D. Wallace Johnson Collection)

Opposite Bottom: C&O's largest terminal and hub in Virginia after Newport News was Clifton Forge, where shops took care of most heavy repair work for locomotives operating on the eastern end of the line. The hump yard was used to classify coal coming in from West Virginia for its final destination at Newport News or elsewhere east. This aerial photo from 1956 shows the main yard with the shops in the upper left and the station and administrative area in lower right. The icing platform is seen next to the Jackson River. The Smith Creek yard is out of sight to the bottom, and the Selma yard beyond the shops in the mist. (C&O Ry. Photo, C&O Hist. Soc. Coll., CSPR-10469.405)

Clifton Forge was the terminal for three major lines and the all kinds of motive power congregated here, both heavy and light. In this evocative 1945 scene 2-8-2s, 2-8-4s, 2-6-6-6s, and others congregate at the ready track for the heavy war-time traffic. (C&O Ry. Photo, C&O Hist. Soc. Coll., CSPR-116)

The Hot Springs Branch ran from Covington to Hot Springs and was built in 1890-91 by C&O to allow it to carry through Pullman cars from New York to the new Homestead Hotel at Hot Springs. It performed this function as an almost all-passenger branch until 1970! In the late years the trains hauled both passenger and freight as needed. Here in 1954 GP9 No. 5829 has such a mixed train on the line nearing Covington with a combination car for the crew and an occasional local passenger, a heavyweight Pullman pool car, a box car and a hopper, and a caboose out of sight. (Robert G. Lewis Photo, TLC Collection)

E-8 No. 4010 and two others power a heavy westbound Train No. 5/47, The Sportsman, at Moss Run, 21 miles west of Clifton Forge on the Alleghany Subdivision, where the steep grade begins, in September 1959. West of Clifton Forge the C&O was double tracked to Cincinnati. The Alleghany Subdivision ran 78 miles from Clifton Forge, Virginia, to Hinton, West Virginia, with 30 miles of the line in Virginia. (C&O Ry. Photo, C&O Hist. Soc. Coll., CSPR-4572)

One of C&O's giant 2-6-6-6 Allegheny types brings a coal train down the grade at Moss Run in December 1948, with lots of brake smoke trailing behind. All the coal from W. Va. and Kentucky that was headed east funneled over this line from Hinton to Clifton Forge and in the late steam era was usually powered by an H-8 on the front and a second one pushing as far as Alleghany (top of the grade). (C&O Ry. Photo, C&O Hist. Soc. Coll., CSPR-2231)

Alleghany was the westernmost station on C&O mainline in Virginia and served as the terminal for the pusher locomotives which helped the heavy coal trains up the grade from Hinton, W. Va. Here the photographer is looking west as H-8 2-6-6-6 No. 1601 has cut off from a coal train (which has left eastbound) and it is moving toward the turntable, where it will turn and be sent back to Hinton. Alleghany Tunnel is out of sight around the curve behind the locomotive. C&O had the easiest eastbound grade for its heavy coal traffic of any of the railroads that hauled West Virginia coal, including B&O, WM, N&W, and Virginian. (B. F. Cutler Photo, C&O Hist. Soc. Coll., COHS-1390)

One of the most important railways which operated in Virginia was the Norfolk & Western. It and its predecessors had an important effect on the state's development from the earliest era of railroads in America. N&W had its corporate and mechanical headquarters at Roanoke, in western Virginia, and was always known and identified as a Virginia railroad. In the era of this book it operated mainly in Virginia, West Virginia, and Ohio, but after merger with the Nickel Plate Road (New York, Chicago & St. Louis) and the Wabash Railroad in the mid-1960s, its reach expanded throughout the Midwest and into the Northeast. Ultimately, in 1991 it merged with the Southern Railway, another line closely identified with Virginia, to form the giant Norfolk Southern Railroad, which today operates a large network in the Southeast, Midwest, and Northeast, including remnants of the older Northeastern roads that were a part of Conrail from the 1970s into the 1990s. The new NS is still a Virginia corporation with its main administrative headquarters in Norfolk.

When one thinks of the Norfolk & Western and its history today, the words coal and steam locomotives are paramount. It was the hauling of this "burning rock" that made the N&W the powerhouse of 20th Century railroading that led to today's giant Norfolk Southern Railroad. Its coal came from fields in southern West Virginia and southwestern Virginia. N&W also became known as one of the nation's premier developers in the art of designing and building steam locomotives. In this regard it was quite similar to two other Virginia Railroads, the Virginian and the Chesapeake & Ohio.

The beginning of what was to become the N&W was the City Point Railroad, which built a line from Petersburg, south of Richmond, about nine miles to City Point on the James River, that most important of Virginia waterways, in 1837-38. Service over the line began on September 7, 1838. This allowed the developing commercial city of Petersburg better access to the James. Previously it had relied on navigation on the shallow Appomattox River. The Petersburg Railroad also built a line from the town southward toward Weldon, North Carolina, a few years before, so Petersburg was well on its way to becoming a transportation hub.

In 1847 the city of Petersburg purchased the City Point Railroad and renamed it the Appomattox Railroad. Unlike many southern railroads, it was built to what would become "standard gauge" of 4-feet, 8-½-inches.

Between 1849 and 1854, as railway technology was gaining headway everywhere, the South Side Railroad was built 123 miles between Petersburg and the fledging industrial and commercial city of Lynchburg, located along the up-

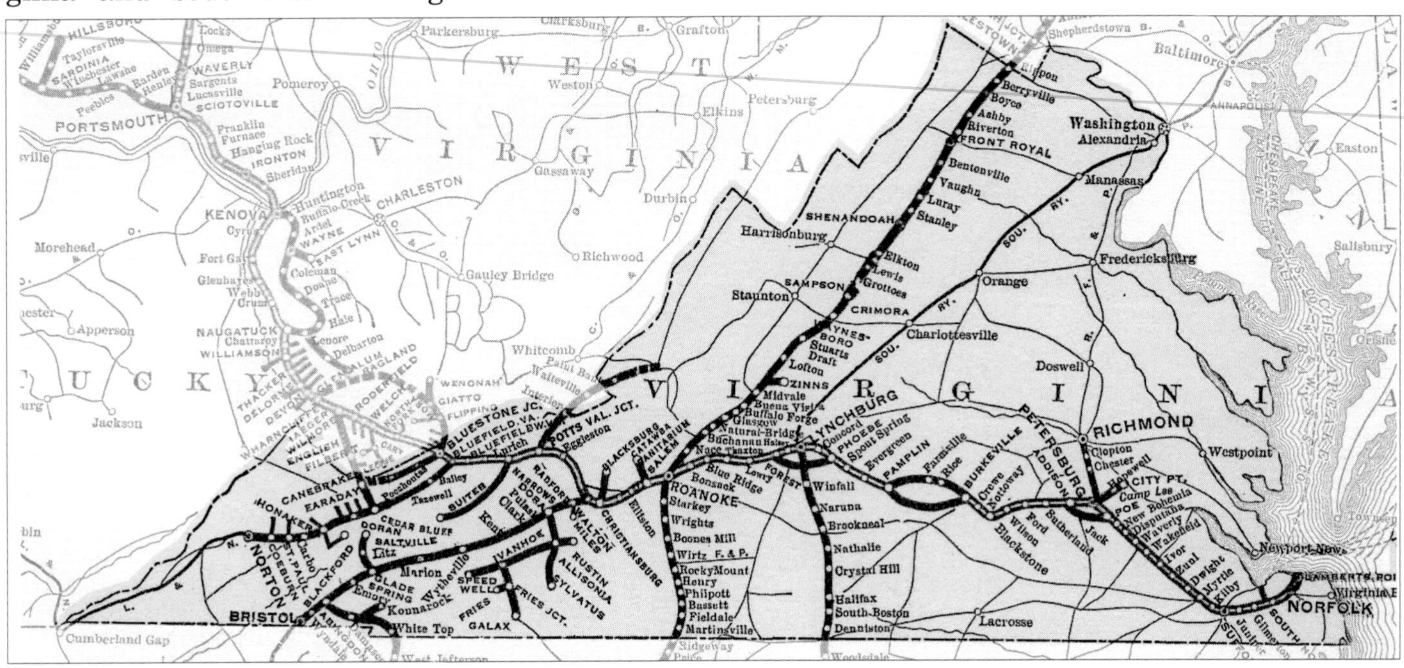

per James River, just east of the Blue Ridge. On May 1, 1854, the Appomattox Railroad (nee City Point) was merged into the new South Side Railroad, giving it access to navigation at City Point. Its gauge was widened to five feet to match that of the South Side. One of the most famous engineering works of this line was the High Bridge across the Appomattox River, a massive structure of some 2,400 feet in length that was considered a major feat in this early era of railroad building.

After building through Farmville, Pamplin, Appomattox, and Concord, the South Side reached the James about six miles downstream of Lynchburg, bridged the river, and ran its line on the north bank to Persival's Island in the river at Lynchburg. Southside established its yard and shop facilities on the large island. A bridge was soon built to connect with the tracks of the Virginia & Tennessee Railroad in Lynchburg proper.

The Virginia & Tennessee was incorporated in 1848 and by October 1856 had completed a line of 204 miles between Lynchburg and Bristol on the Virginia/Tennessee border. Its eastern terminal at Lynchburg connected with the old James River & Kanawha Canal (which supplied the main transport between Richmond and Lynchburg from about 1840) and then connected with the newly completed South Side Railroad. At Bristol it connected with the East Tennessee and Virginia Railroad (later Southern Railway) to Knoxville. It also was built to 5-foot gauge.

The other key line in the early development of N&W's predecessors was the Norfolk & Petersburg railroad. Work began in 1853 along the 80 miles between the two cities. Fifty-two miles of the road consisted of an absolutely straight line. Most difficult in its construction was its passage through the Great Dismal Swamp, which required extraordinary work to build the track on a suitable roadbed. The road was opened on April 13, 1858. It made a connection with the South Side in Petersburg, and the newspaper boasted that the ". . .waters of the Atlantic and the Mississippi will be connected together by a continuous line of railway of unbroken gauge. . . ."

This was the situation when the War Between the States intervened, causing great havoc in Virginia and ruining much of the railway infrastructure in the state.

After the war, William Mahone, who began as the Chief Engineer of the Norfolk & Petersburg, and served as a Confederate General, was elected president of the Norfolk & Petersburg, the South Side, and the Virginia and Tennessee, and under his guidance the three companies were merged into the new Atlantic, Mississippi & Ohio Railroad in November 1870.

With the creation of the AM&O, what was to become the N&W main line in Virginia was essentially complete. Mahone's tempestuous career with the AM&O alienated many and after the financial panic of 1873 and the following depression, the company finally passed into the hands of a receiver in 1876.

During this time C. H. Clark, a financier from Philadelphia, was building a railroad down the Shenandoah Valley from Hagerstown, Maryland, to connect with the AM&O at Big Lick, Virginia (later Roanoke). He purchased the AM&O at foreclosure and on May 3, 1881, and the name was changed to Norfolk & Western Railroad. Clark was concerned not only to provide his Shenandoah Valley Railroad* with a friendly connection, but also wanted to develop the coal fields located to the west of Roanoke in southwestern Virginia and southern West Virginia.

The Shenandoah Valley line failed to stand alone and went into bankruptcy in 1885. It was purchased at foreclosure by N&W in 1890 and became the Shenandoah Division. This line proved highly valuable as the N&W's connection to the great traffic base to and from the Northeastern states.

The new owners extended the N&W 75 miles westward toward New River beginning in 1883,

*When the Shenandoah Valley and the N&W "connected" they were built to different gauges (4' 8-½" for Shenandoah, and 5' for N&W), so a hoist had to be built at Roanoke, which lifted cars from one line and set them on the trucks compatible with the other line. This was the case at many locations throughout to country since many railroads, especially in the South, had been built to a gauge broader than the common 4' 8-½" used in the North. Finally in 1886, on a single day, all the non-standard gauge railroads in the South were changed to standard gauge, and forever afterward the standard 4' 8-½" has ruled in the United States, and in most of the world.

N&W Coal Pier No. 4 at Lambert's Point, Norfolk, with collier Aboukir, *obviously taking coal for export. The pier worked in this way: hoppers of coal came into the yard and were dumped into the large electric cars (see one at end of pier), which were then carried by elevator to the top of the pier. Once on the top they ran along the platform (using electric trolley line) and dumped the coal into ships through chutes. The C&O had a similar pier on the Newport News side. This was replaced by a much more modern dumper-conveyor system. (N&W Railway Photo, TLC Collection)*

At the same time that N&W was building its coal transfer piers at Norfolk, the Chesapeake & Ohio (C&O), running across Virginia north of the N&W route, extended its line in the east from Richmond to Newport News on the great deepwater port of Hampton Roads, opposite Norfolk. At Newport News the C&O also erected a pier for dumping coal into barges and ships bound for Northeastern cities. The two railways competed in shipping coal from these two terminals the balance of their lives and into the era of their successors down to the present day. After the Virginian Railway built its piers at Sewalls Point on the Norfolk side in 1909, it became the third competitor in this trade.

Meanwhile, C&O and N&W competed for the westbound coal business, since Virginian had no westward lines, handing its westbound coal over to NYC or C&O. N&W attempted to acquire the Virginian in the mid-1920s but was unable to do so, but finally, in 1959 it merged Virginian, and used some of its better grades for the eastbound coal business.

reaching to what is now Bluefield, Virginia/West Virginia, and the new mining town of Pocahontas. The first car of what was to become the famous "Pocahontas" coal traveled over N&W on March 12, 1883, and in the balance of that year N&W handled over 80,000 tons of coal.

To handle coal bound for the northeast, N&W built a five-mile line to Lambert's Point near Norfolk, where piers were erected for transfer of coal from railway to barges and ships. This was the beginning of the great coal pier transfer operations that continue to this day at that point. These piers were constantly rebuilt, enlarged, expanded, and their capacity increased as export coal became a more important element in the market in the mid-20th century.

In 1883 a large General Office building was erected at Roanoke, and this remained the headquarters of the line until the NS merger in the early 1980s when the headquarters was moved to Norfolk.

A 45-mile branch was built to what is now Pulaski, Virginia, mainly to reach iron ore deposits. At that time it was thought that Virginia's iron ore production was to become more important than it actually ever did. This line was later extended 52 miles to Galax, again to haul iron ore. Then, in 1887 the Clinch Valley extension was built from

N&W's more modern coal pier is seen here in 1936 filling up the steamer Isaac T. Mann *undoubtedly for coastwise transport to the northeastern U. S. Isaac T. Mann was an early coal operator in the Pocahontas fields. Note that the hopper car is elevated and rotated to dump its contents directly into the ship. (Eastern Coal Archives Collection)*

Graham (Bluefield, Va.) into the coal fields of southwestern Virginia, running about 100 miles through Tazewell, Richlands, and southwest to Norton, Virginia. This line became a junction point with the Clinchfield Railroad when it was built south from Elkhorn City, Kentucky, crossing the N&W again at St. Paul, Virginia.

At Norton a connection was made with the Louisville & Nashville's coal lines from Kentucky. The Clinch Valley extension of the N&W became an important coal producing area.

In 1890 N&W gained control of the Scioto Valley Railroad from Portsmouth to Columbus, in Ohio, hoping to eventually use it as a westward extension, but it did not physically connect with N&W at all.

In 1891-92 the 191-mile gap through West Virginia was completed, including a bridge across the Ohio River at Kenova, West Virginia. This gave N&W a western outlet for its coal and a competitive advantage over C&O, which had western connections at Cincinnati, but no good route to Great Lakes shipping in Ohio. During the 1890s and well into the 20th Century, many branches were built in southwestern Virginia and West Virginia to reach the rich coal seams that lay beneath the mountains of these regions, and the coal business expanded exponentially.

To improve its operations, N&W established a division point yard at Crewe, in Nottoway County about half-way along the 258-mile line between Roanoke and Norfolk in 1888. Here it erected a large roundhouse and machine shop for locomotive repair and servicing, and a yard mainly to accommodate coal being staged eastward for the Lambert's Point pier. This eliminated Petersburg and Lynchburg as division points and shop areas. In 1892 a large terminal yard and roundhouse was built at Shenandoah, about half-way on the Shenandoah Valley line (Roanoke to Shenandoah was 133 miles, Shenandoah to Hagerstown was 103 miles).

In this same era of expansion (1892) N&W leased the Roanoke & Southern Railway, which became its line from Roanoke to Winston-Salem, North Carolina, and that same year acquired the Lynchburg & Durham Railroad, reaching to the latter point in North Carolina.

Although the expansions were obviously needed, the expenditures were too great and when the financial panic of 1893 occurred N&W was again thrown into receivership. In 1896 the line emerged from receivership as the Norfolk & Western Rail<u>way</u> (vice the previous Rail<u>road</u>).

By 1901 the Pennsylvania Railroad had acquired control of both N&W and C&O in order to eliminate the competition that West Virginia coal from these two lines, shipped to the northeast via Hampton Roads, was creating for the Pennsylvania's own on-line coal. C&O and N&W coal was actually cheaper in the big cities than the PRR's coal, hauled a much shorter distance. However, this opened up the Great Lakes traffic for N&W through its coal being routed over the PRR north of Columbus.

PRR retained control of C&O for only a few years, but held its N&W interests until 1964. Though PRR didn't exercise much direct control over operations in later years, its influence manifested itself in the signaling systems that were similar to PRR's and the Tuscan Red color of N&W's passenger cars, which was a standard of the PRR.

In 1901 N&W acquired its line from Portsmouth to Cincinnati (built originally in the 1880s as the narrow gauge Cincinnati, Portsmouth & Virginia Railroad), as well as numerous other short lines. One of the major changes of the era was the complete realignment of N&W's route from Naugatuck to Kenova, in southern West Virginia. The main line was relocated and built with better grades and curvature, hugging the Tug Fork and Big Sandy rivers which formed the border between Kentucky and West Virginia.

In 1901 as well the Lambert's Point coal terminal was improved with Pier No. 3. In 1902 a belt line bypassing the congested line through the city of Lynchburg was completed, allowing a better routing for through freight than via the original route. This lower grade line of 23 miles ran from Forest, just west of Lynchburg, to Phoebe, near Concord, where it rejoined the old line. It mainly allowed through eastbound coal trains to completely bypass Lynchburg and was occasionally used for westbound service. A similar belt line was opened at Petersburg in 1911, again primarily used for eastbound coal trains. In 1916 another, better grade line of 37 miles between Burkeville and Pamplin was completed, bypassing Farmville.

The Farmville Belt followed an original Southside RR survey that was not used in favor of the Farmville line in the 1850s. It also was primarily used for eastbound coal.

With its huge cash reserves from coal business, N&W rebuilt its roadway, tunnels, terminals, shops, yards, and other facilities so that by the 1920s they were among the best in the country. N&W became legendary as the consummate practitioner of the locomotive builder's art. Its talented managers and workers turned out some of the best steam locomotives of all time in the following decades. To complement this, N&W began probably the best use of steam by any railroad, tailoring its locomotives to its particular needs, so that by the post-WWII era, when all other railroads were rushing headlong into dieselization as fast as they could, N&W continued building steam. It was the last Class I railroad in America to dieselize, and didn't drop the fires of its last steamers until early May 1960. This was possible because N&W used its ultramodern and very versatile steam much as other roads used their diesels, dispatching and servicing them on a turn-around time that was equal to diesels. But eventually, as good as N&W steam was, it had to fall to diesels for many reasons.

N&W recognized the efficiency of electric operations and between 1916 and 1923 installed electric operations over 55 miles of its West Virginia mainline as well as some branches. The only place where electric lines touched Virginia was in the few miles around Pocahontas, where the main line west of Bluefield crossed the state line briefly.

Roanoke Shops

In 1883, Roanoke Machine Works began to build locomotives for the N&W. This company was then merged into N&W in 1897 and became its famous Roanoke Shops. In the following decades this facility was steadily improved and expanded, and although N&W continued to buy locomotives from the commercial builders, it built many itself in these large shops. After 1927 N&W purchased no locomotives from outside builders and built all of its new engines at Roanoke. The Roanoke shop became famous not only because it was probably the largest locomotive building operation carried on by an individual railroad, but because it concentrated on developing the standard steam locomotive types to their highest degree of efficiency. It produced its last locomotive in 1952, four years after the last commercially built steamer in the U. S. After the closing of the Richmond Works of the American Locomotive Company in 1927, N&W Shop was the only locomotive builder in the South. It built 152 new locomotives for N&W between 1883 and 1897 and 295 between 1895 and 1952.

J-class No. 611 is about to depart Norfolk's Terminal Station with a westbound train the early 1950s, as the office tower portion of the terminal rises in the background. All N&W trains began their westward trek from this location. (TLC Collection)

In the 1914–1920 period, the flow of coal westward greatly increased so that it eventually became much larger than the original eastward traffic. Eastbound traffic increased after World War II, when demand for export coal grew.

Coal branches were built in southern West Virginia and southwestern Virginia in the era after 1900, resulting in ever increasing amounts of coal being hauled by N&W. The Pocahontas Coal Field, which took its name from the N&W town of Pocahontas, covered this region and the operational make-up on the N&W overlapped these two states as well as a few miles in Kentucky.

In the era up to the 1960s, N&W concentrated much of its attention on its operations in the coal fields of southwestern Virginia and West Virginia, and it was only as it began to buy other railroads in the Midwest that it began to become a more diversified operation.

By 1964 N&W encompassed its original line, the Virginian (merged 1959), plus the Nickel Plate Railroad (merged 1964), Wabash Railroad (merged 1964), Akron, Canton & Youngstown Railroad (merged 1982), Atlantic & Danville Railroad (merged 1962), and others, which had been acquired in the 1960s. In 1991 N&W merged with the Southern Railway to form Norfolk Southern, the company which now operates the former N&W and Virginian lines in Virginia. NS eventually acquired portions of Conrail, mainly the former Pennsylvania Railroad lines in a twist of ironic fate that had an N&W-dominated NS triumphant over PRR.

Because the lines overlapped the West Virginia/Virginia border, it is somewhat difficult and actually an artificial device to separate them based on geography. Even though the Pocahontas Division was headquartered in Bluefield, W. Va., it operated numerous lines in Virginia. - The table below will give a generalized overview of N&W lines in Virginia and the accompanying map will show how they interfaced with the West Virginia lines.

Most of N&W's lines west of Roanoke were operated for coal production. Of course, the mainline from Norfolk to Cincinnati and Columbus also hosted a number of through fast freights and passenger trains.

Though N&W's prime income and major operational concern was coal and other freight business, it did have a modest but well operated and extensively advertised passenger service. The mainline trains ran between Norfolk and Cincinnati. In the mid-20th century era of this book, the three main named trains on the route were the *Powhatan Arrow*, the *Pocahontas*, and the *Cavalier*. Mainline locals also operated into the 1950s. Trains with through cars to New York via the Pennsylvania Railroad connection at Hagerstown operated over the Shenandoah Valley line, and numerous branch trains handled folks bound to and from the coal fields towns. The mixed train on the Abington branch became rather famous because it lasted very late and was photographed by many railfans. The "Virginia Creeper" train on the Blacksburg Branch is fondly remembered for transporting the students to and from Virginia Polytechnic Institute (now known as "Virginia Tech"). Although N&W did not have a line to Richmond, it operated connecting passenger trains over the 25 miles or so between Petersburg and Richmond by trackage arrangement with the Atlantic Coast Line.

This photo at Myrtle, on N&W's arrow-straight line between Petersburg and Norfolk has one of the road's magnificent A-class simple 2-6-6-4s which were so effectively used in this region. It has an auxiliary water tender which extended its operating range. Note that though this is a coal train it has some general freight up front, often the case in the 1950s, when this photo was taken. (H. Reid Photo, TLC Collection)

Class Z-1b No. 1444 on a westbound local freight near Petersburg July 5, 1947. N&W stabled a respectable number of 2-6-6-2 compounds which were used in coal train and local traffic on the eastern end of the system. (August Thieme Photo, TLC Collection)

N&W 4-6-2 No. 563 is on the head of ACL Train No. 25, one of the passenger trains that operated over the Atlantic Coast Line between N&W's mainline at Petersburg, and Richmond's Broad Street Station (in the background). Although operated as ACL trains, they usually consisted of an N&W locomotive and cars except for an ACL baggage car/express. The coaches will be added to N&W No. 4, The Pocahontas, *at Petersburg. (J.R. Quinn Photo, TLC Collection)*

Diesel-powered No. 3, the westbound Pocahontas, *pauses in December 1962 at Crewe. The town, named for a great railroad center in England, was created in 1888 by N&W to provide a terminal between Roanoke and Norfolk, breaking up the long run on the Norfolk Division. It had a 21-stall engine house, coaling station, and the usual terminal facilities, and a large yard, mainly for staging eastbound coal. When N&W dieselized in 1958 the EMD model E-units were no longer in regular production, so N&W settled for the ugly non-streamlined GP9s for its passenger power. (Curt Tillotson Photo, TLC Collection)*

Typical of N&W's higher-class type of passenger station built around the turn of the 20th Century is Bedford, about 30 miles east of Roanoke, a town of only a couple thousand people, but the seat of Bedford County. Stations similar to this somewhat odd and eclectic design appear at numerous N&W locations in Virginia. (N&W Photo, TLC Collection

A-Class simple articulated 2-6-6-4 No. 1242 is powering a westbound empty coal train toward the Blue Ridge at Villamont in 1954. The A Class was one of N&W's trio of modern steam power that it developed to a high pinnacle of efficiency in the 1930 and 1950s. A "Super Power" locomotive by any standard, the A-Class was used on fast freight and coal trains just about anywhere on the N&W system. (John Krause Photo, TLC Collection)

One of N&W's giant compound articulated 2-8-8-2s, Y-6 class No. 2130 rests in the Roanoke engine terminal area (Shaffer's Crossing engine terminal) in July 1956. N&W developed its 2-8-8-2 types over forty years from 1910 until the last were built in 1952, and used them in all types of service long after the compound type had lost favor with other railroads and steam builders. (Joe Schmitz Photo, TLC Collection)

Power was needed to lift eastbound coal trains over the Blue Ridge. Here Y-6 No. 2167 leads an A-class, while a third locomotive pushes in the distance out of sight. (Railroad Ave. Enterprises)

One of the pushers on the Blue Ridge grade shoves hard on the rear of a coal train that has quite a few Clinchfield hoppers in consist. These undoubtedly came from that road at its principal N&W connection at St. Paul in far southwest Virginia. (TLC Collection)

This great N&W publicity photo posed a fleet of the railway's best steam locomotives at the Shaffer's Crossing engine terminal in Roanoke in the early 1950s. The two long structures on each side of the photos are the "luboratoria" that provided for quick servicing of locomotives without moving them from one station to another. The roundhouse is in the background. A-class and Y-class engines dominate, with a J-class 4-8-4 in the right lubratorium. (N&W Photo, TLC Collection)

N&W 4-8-2 No. 107, fairly shining in this publicity photo, is riding the turntable at the Shaffer's crossing roundhouse in Roanoke. N&W was famous for the big Class-A and Y freight locomotives, but had a large stable of 4-8-2s and unusual 4-8-0s that handled local business and other traffic that didn't entail the height of the coal trains and the through freights. (N&W Photo, TLC Collection)

J-Class No. 608, one of the streamlined 4-8-4s, probably the most famous N&W locomotive type, is seen here powering No. 4, The Pocahontas through the Roanoke yard on July 18, 1958 the last regularly scheduled train hauled by steam. (N&W Photo, TLC Collection)

Streamlined 4-8-2 Mountain type (Class K-2) is seen here in July 1956, in the Roanoke lubratorium as workers busy themselves lubricating and servicing the engine during the process of turning it. The lubratorium was set up so that a locomotive could be parked in the building and then all the oils and greases that were required could be applied by hoses strategically placed, so that it didn't have to be moved. This was part of N&W's highly efficient steam locomotive utilization. (Joe Schmitz Photo)

Although not one of the steam locomotives most often associated with the N&W, one of its 4-8-2 Mountain types is seen here at the Shenandoah engine terminal. These locomotives saw a good deal of service on the Shenandoah Division. This photo was taken Sept, 5, 1954. (TLC Collection)

This page: N&W's main passenger station was at Roanoke. It was remodeled from an older structure by famed industrial designer Raymond Loewy and accommodated N&W's main line name trains operating between Norfolk and Cincinnati, as well as the Southern's trains operating over the N&W on their runs between Washington and Memphis/New Orleans.

The modernistic façade added by Loewy to replace an old one with classic columns. (W. E. Warden Photo, TLC Collection)

Inside, Loewy appointed the station with the best of Mid-Century Modern design including this stylish ticketing area with system map. (N&W Photo, TLC Collection)

The rear of the station shows the new concourse extending over the tracks and the canopies below. - The station was used as offices after the end of passenger service, but today houses the O. Winston Link Museum. (TLC Collection)

Y-3 class 2081 and others engines congregate around the coaling station at Shenandoah in 1956. The terminal at Shenandoah was about midway on the Shenandoah Division running between Roanoke and Hagerstown, Md. (TLC Collection)

J Class No. 607 pops out of the tunnel near Pembroke with a passenger train in 1950. This was always a favorite haunt for N&W publicity photographers as well as railfans because of its scenery. (H. Reid Photo, TLC Collection)

One unusual aspect of N&W passenger service was the transport of Southern Railway trains between Monroe (Lynchburg), and Bristol. Here No. 46, Southern's Tennessean, is seen at Glenvar, on April 3, 1946 with J Class 602 for power. The SR's stainless steel cars contrast with N&W's red cars in the consist. Later, after N&W dieselized, SR diesels ran through, but while N&W was still steam, there were no diesel servicing facilities for the trip through Virginia. (N&W Photo, TLC Collection)

The famous N&W steam-turbine-electric No. 2300 "Jawn Henry" tackles Christiansburg grade in August 1954, with a westbound freight. Note the men in the coal bin area on the locomotive's nose. C&O tried the turbines in 1948 in an effort to marry the efficiency of electric drive with coal fuel, but quickly gave up. N&W tried six years later with better results, but still the diesel was better and would eventually win, even on N&W. (E. P. Street Photo, H. H. Harwood, Jr. Collection)

Also along New River, a brace of four EMD GP9 diesels has an empty train westbound at Pearisburg with a fairly large cut of general freight up front, in about 1959. N&W was the last Class I railroad to dieselize and when it did most of its first fleet consisted of GP9s, used both for passenger and freight service. (N&W Photo, TLC Collection)

The famous "Huckleberry" mixed train operated up the branch from Christiansburg to Blacksburg and became famous for carrying students from mainline trains to Virginia Polytechnic Institute (Virginia Tech) in this fine old combination car, seen here in June 1958, parked beside the Christiansburg station. No. 405 was one of N&W's unusual 4-8-0 types. (H. H. Harwood, Jr. Photo)

Pocahontas Fuel Company's Pocahontas tipple is typical of many that operated on N&W lines in southwest Virginia. Pocahontas is on a very short branch line extending from Bluestone Junction in West Virginia, across the border into Virginia a distance of only 1-½ miles. (TLC Collection)

This is the three-car local train on the Clinch Valley line out of Bluefield to Norton, in the coal areas of far southwestern Virginia in June of 1958. At the very end of steam, 4-6-2 No. 578 is in charge, including an auxiliary tender of which N&W made such good use. (J. Parker Lamb Photo)

The automatic coaling machine is being used in this March, 1957 photo, to replenish the fuel on J Class No. 604 at Bristol. The big J has just brought in one of the through Southern Railway trains and will have to be readied at the small terminal to take the next one back north to Monroe. (L.D. Lewis Collection)

On March 2, 1957, N&W Y-6 class 2-8-8-2 No. 2145 brings an extra freight train south into Bristol, Virginia. N&W terminated at the Virginia/Tennessee border, and handed its through business over to the Southern Railway. The compound 2-8-8-2 Y-classes were the general purpose locomotive of N&W and could be seen almost everywhere on its system. (L.D. Lewis Collection)

Southern Railway

The Southern Railway Company, which operated over 6,000 miles of road, was the product of nearly 150 predecessor railroads that were combined by various reorganizations, mergers and consolidations to form a 13 state system. "The Southern Serves the South" was aptly chosen by the company as its advertising slogan and Fairfax Harrison, a former president of the Southern, liked to say that the slogan was really a statement of fact. Its lines traversed every state (except West Virginia) in the territory south of the Ohio and Potomac and east of the Mississippi rivers, serving nearly every community of importance in the South. Its lines even reached into the states of Indiana and Illinois. Its northern gateways were located at Washington (Potomac Yard) and Cincinnati. Western gateways were located at St. Louis and Memphis. Its lines also reached the tidewater ports at Norfolk, Charleston, Savannah, Brunswick and Jacksonville on the Atlantic seaboard, and Mobile and New Orleans on the Gulf coast.

The incorporation of the Southern Railway was effected by an act of the General Assembly of Virginia in 1894. The company was formed for the purpose of acquiring the property and assets of the Richmond and West Point Terminal Railway and Warehouse Company, a holding company and its controlled companies, including what was then known as the Richmond and Danville Railroad Company System and East Tennessee, Virginia and Georgia Railway Company System, which had all gone through a protracted period of bankruptcy.

The Southern operated 970 miles of line in the Commonwealth of Virginia, connecting its communities with the principal industrial and agricultural sections of the South. At Danville, three lines converged – one from Washington via Alexandria, Charlottesville and Lynchburg; one from West Point via Richmond; and one (via lease of the Atlantic and Danville Railway, from Pinners Point, opposite Norfolk on Hampton Roads. The line from Washington to Danville, a distance of 235 miles, was the northern portion of the 637-mile Washington to Atlanta main line. A branch line off the Washington to Danville main line at Manassas operated to Harrisonburg and served the Shenandoah Valley. A branch line off the Richmond to Danville main line at Keysville operated via Clarksville to Durham, North Carolina. The Appalachia Division extended west from Bristol and served the coal fields of southwest Vir-

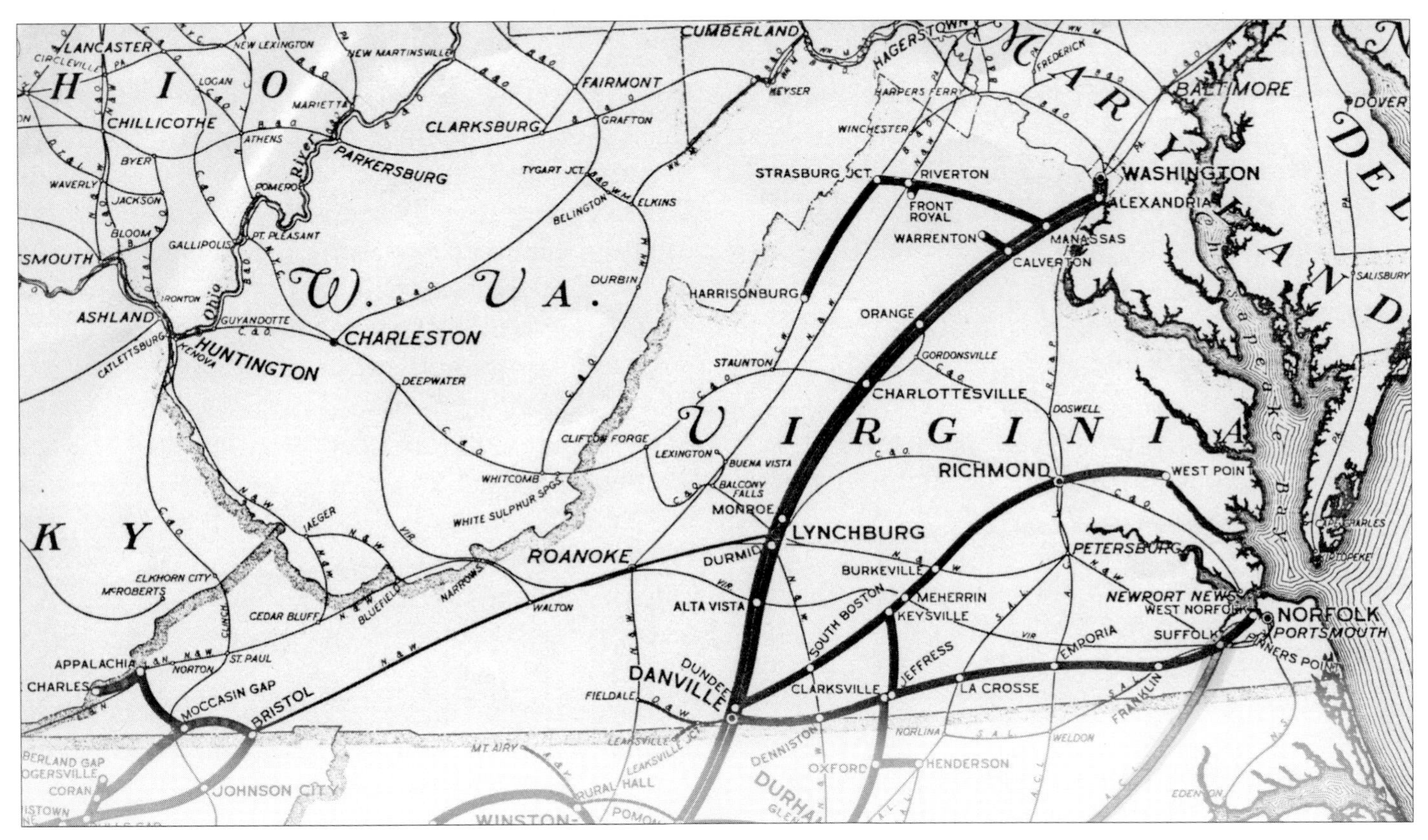

Southern Railway Class Ps-4 Pacific No. 1395 is southbound from Alexandria in May of 1938 with Train No. 35, the The Washington-Atlanta-New Orleans Express. In the 1930's, No. 35 offered coach, drawing room sleeping car and air conditioned dining car service. The best known of the Southern's Pacific 4-6-2 type steam locomotives, the Ps-4's were first delivered to the railroad in 1923 by Schenectady Locomotive Works. The original locomotives were so successful on the Washington to Atlanta passenger runs that additional locomotives were ordered between 1924 and 1928. The first Ps-4's in the Southern's distinctive green, gold and silver paint scheme were built by Richmond and arrived in 1926. The Southern Ps-4's were numbered in the series 1366-1409. PS-4's in the 6000 number series also worked on the Southern's CNOT&TP and the AGS lines. (W. H. Thrall Photo/Frank E. Ardrey, Jr. Collection)

ginia. The Southern also operated into Pinners Point by way of Suffolk over the ACL's line from Selma, North Carolina as the result of a trackage rights agreement between the two roads.

The Southern also owned or leased the lines of several railroads that operated in the Commonwealth of Virginia. It had an ownership interest in and later acquired the Danville and Western Railway, the Interstate Railroad, and the Norfolk Southern Railway. For a period of time it leased the Atlantic and Danville Railway and the Bluemont Branch of the Washington and Old Dominion Railway. It had an ownership interest in the Norfolk and Portsmouth Belt Line Railroad and the Richmond, Fredericksburg and Potomac Railroad and was a tenant at Potomac Yard. The history of these railroads and the Southern's interest therein are discussed in other chapters of this book. In this chapter we will focus on the principal lines operated by the Southern Railway in the Commonwealth.

The Southern Railway main line between Washington and Danville was built by several historic railroads that for a period of time were under the control of the Baltimore and Ohio Railroad. The oldest of these lines was the Orange and Alexandria Railroad. This railroad was chartered in 1848 by businessmen in the city of Alexandria who were concerned by their port's loss of trade to the port of Baltimore. The Winchester and Potomac Railroad had been built in the upper Shenandoah Valley to connect with the B&O RR at Harper's Ferry, enabling goods to be shipped from the valley to Baltimore via the W&P RR and the B&O RR.

Construction of the O&A RR began in 1850 and it reached Tudor Hall (now Manassas) in 1851. The line was completed to Gordonsville in 1854 where it made a connection with the Virginia Central Railroad (predecessor of the Chesapeake and Ohio Railway) and the O&A RR acquired trackage rights over the VC RR from Gordonsville to Charlottesville. The O&A RR then built its own extension from Charlottesville to Lynchburg, reaching that city in 1860. The O&A RR was off to a grand start, but its fortunes were soon altered by the War Between the States. Given its strategic location near Washington, the northern portion of the line was captured by the Union army and was operated during the war by the U. S. Military RR. Following the war, the B&O began to acquire control of the O&A RR. In 1867, it was merged into the Manassas Gap RR to form the Orange, Alexandria and Manassas RR. In 1872, the OA&M RR was merged with the Lynchburg and Danville Railroad to form a new company known as the Virginia and North Carolina Railroad. On the date of merger, the V&NC

owned about 285 miles of line, which included 61 miles from the OA&M RR; 159 miles from the O&A RR; and, 65 miles of partially constructed line from the L&D extending from Lynchburg to Neapolis. The following year, the V&NC RR was renamed the Washington City, Virginia Midland and Great Southern Railroad. In 1876, the Charlottesville and Rapidan Railroad was organized to build a direct line for the WC, VM and GS RR between Orange and Charlottesville. Completed in 1880, this cutoff from Orange to Charlottesville via Barboursville tied together the main line and the trains of the WC,VM & GS no longer needed to use the C&O line from Gordonsville to Charlottesville. However, the railroad had gone into bankruptcy in 1876 and was operated by a receiver until 1881 when control of the railroad passed to the B&O, which reorganized the railroad and renamed it the Virginia Midland Railroad. The Virginia Midland was leased by the B&O to the Richmond and Danville Railroad in 1886 and in 1891, the Virginia Midland granted the C&O trackage rights over its line from Orange to Alexandria. In 1894 both the Virginia Midland and the Richmond and Danville RR became a part of the new Southern Railway.

In discussing the history of the Orange and Alexandria RR above, mention was made of the Manassas Gap Railroad. This railroad was the predecessor company of the Southern Railway's Harrisonburg Branch. Following Alexandria's initial success in chartering the Orange and Alexandria RR, the city decided to extend the rail line into the Shenandoah Valley. In 1850, the city obtained a charter to build the Manassas Gap Railroad from "...some convenient point on the Orange and Alexandria Railroad, through Manassas Gap, passing near the town of Strasburg, to the town of Harrisonburg in the county of Rockingham". An agreement was reached for the Manassas Gap RR to operate its trains over the O&A RR between Tudor Hall (now Manassas) and Alexandria. Construction commenced in 1851 with the line was completed to The Plains in 1852; Linden in 1853; Strasburg in 1854; and, Mt. Jackson in 1858. A branch line was built to reach Front Royal. Further construction of the railroad ceased during the War Between the States and by the end of the war the railroad had been totally destroyed. In 1867, the Manassas Gap RR was merged with the O&A RR to form the Orange, Alexandria and Manassas RR, which completed construction of the line from Mt. Jackson to Harrisonburg. Trains began to run into Harrisonburg on January 15, 1869. When the OA&M RR was merged into the Lynchburg & Danville RR, the Manassas Gap RR became a part of the Virginia and North Carolina RR and then, a part of the renamed company, the Washington City, Virginia Midland and Great Southern RR, which was renamed again 1881 as the Virginia Midland. However, in 1873, the portion of the former Manassas Gap RR from Strasburg to Harrisonburg, about 50 miles, was leased to and solely operated by the B&O

Southern Railway Class Ps-4 Pacific No. 1370 with Train No. 18, the Birmingham Special, *crosses over at CR Tower from Southern tracks to reach those of the RF&P at AF Tower in February of 1937. In a few minutes the train will be arriving for its station stop at Alexandria and then on Washington Union Station. Southern's name passenger trains such as the* Crescent Limited, *the* Birmingham Special, *the* Piedmont Limited, *and the* Washington-Atlanta-New Orleans Express *operated over the Washington and Danville divisions in Virginia. (W. H. Thrall Photo/Frank E. Ardrey, Jr. Collection)*

An unidentified Southern Railway Ps-4 Pacific brings its southbound passenger train to a stop at the station in downtown Orange. The Southern Railway line at Orange dates from 1876 when the Charlottesville and Rapidan Railroad was chartered to construct a direct line between Orange and Charlottesville. This line was merged into the Southern and continues to serve as the main line for the Norfolk Southern Corporation between those two cities. (William E. Griffin, Jr. Collection)

RR, which then extended the rail line south to Lexington. However, the Strasburg to Harrisonburg portion of the Branch was returned to the Southern when the B&O went bankrupt in 1896.

Prior to the opening of the Alexandria Union Passenger Station in 1905, the Southern Railway passenger trains operated from a station on the southwest corner Duke and Henry Streets. The Washington Southern Railroad (which was at that time wholly owned by the Pennsylvania Railroad) operated a passenger and freight station in Alexandria on property bounded by Henry, Cameron, Fayette and Queen Streets. The tracks of the Washington Southern joined those of the Southern at Duke and Henry Streets. The main lines of the two railroads departed Alexandria in a southwesterly direction on separate tracks paralleling Duke Street. During this period, South Washington was literally a maze of railroads. From the north end of the Long Bridge to south of the Capitol were the freight yards of the Pennsylvania Railroad and the Southern Railway. There was a freight station and the B&O's freight yards and depot were in the vicinity of Ninth Street and Maryland Avenue.

Substantial changes were made in the railroad operations in the Washington and Alexandria area after the turn of the century. The Richmond-Washington Company was created in 1901 when the Pennsylvania Railroad gave up control of the Washington Southern Railroad and its operation was turned over to the RF&P. On September 15, 1905, the new Alexandria Passenger Station was opened for joint use by the Southern, C&O and Washington Southern. On August 1, 1906, Potomac Yard was opened between the Long Bridge and the northern city limits of Alexandria to eliminate the numerous freight yards in the District of Columbia. The Southern tracks connected with those of the Washington Southern at AF Tower and both the Southern and the C&O were granted trackage rights to Potomac Yard for their freight trains and to the Long Bridge for their passenger trains. The new Washington Terminal Union Passenger Station was opened in the District of Columbia in 1907 and by August 1st of that year, the entire Washington Southern had been doubled tracked from Quantico to the Long Bridge. Washington Terminal became the northern terminal for the Southern's passenger trains and Potomac Yard the northern terminal for its freight trains. As a result of these improvements, traffic substantially increased over the Southern's line from Washington to Atlanta resulting in the double tracking of the line. The first double track of the Southern's line in Virginia was completed between Alexandria and Orange between 1901 and 1904. By 1917, the entire Washington to Charlotte, North Carolina main line was double track until 1962, when the Southern returned selected segments to single track. Centralized traffic control would be installed on the line in the 1950's.

The Harrisonburg Branch would remain a single track line operated by the manual block system.

Until the establishment of the Southern Railway's Eastern Division in 1964, the main line between Washington and Danville was divided into two operating divisions. The dividing point of the two divisions was located at Monroe, a few miles north of the James River. The Washington Division directed operations between Washington and Monroe. This division also included the branch line from Calverton to Warrenton and the Harrisonburg Branch. Operations between Monroe and Danville were under the supervision of the Danville Division. The Southern constructed a new yard at Monroe that was named for a local landowner. Opened on July 4, 1897, the yard was in continuous operation until closed by the Norfolk Southern Corporation in 1985. Monroe was also the away-from-home-terminal for Southern crews operating on both the Washington and Danville divisions.

A number of Southern Railway lines converged at Danville. Just north of the Dan River, at a location known as Dundee, the Southern's double track main line of the Danville Division was joined by the Southern's Richmond to Danville single track main line (the Richmond Division). The Richmond Division main line joined the Danville Division main line at Dundee Tower. Also located at Dundee were a yard office, freight yard, freight house and roundhouse. Steam locomotives were serviced and given running repairs at the Dundee engine house. When the Southern dieselized its motive power, a new diesel shop was built at Dundee in 1950 to service and maintain the diesels of the Southern, Atlantic & Danville Railway and the Danville & Western Railway. The Southern's passenger station was located in the

Southern Railway No. 4839, an Ms-4 class 2-8-2, slows to stop its freight train at Orange in April of 1938. Of the eight classes of 2-8-2's owned by the Southern, the Ms-4 class came to be the standard main line freight locomotives in the later years of steam operation. They were numbered in the series 4800-4914 and were first delivered to the railroad by Richmond Locomotive Works in 1923. They operated primarily on the main line between Alexandria and Atlanta, but eventually were found on lines throughout the system. (W. H. Thrall, Jr. Photo/ Frank E. Ardrey, Jr. Collection)

city of Danville, south of the Dan River and eight tenths of a mile south of Dundee Tower. This station served all of the Southern's passenger trains including those of the Washington to Atlanta main line, the Richmond Division, and those of the Atlantic & Danville Railway's Norfolk to Danville line during the Southern's fifty year lease of the A&D from 1899 to 1949. The tracks of the A&D joined the Southern's Washington to Danville main line at the passenger station. During the period of the lease, the A&D was first operated as Southern's Norfolk Division and in 1930 it became a part of the Southern's Richmond Division. The tracks of the Danville & Western Railway, a wholly owned Southern subsidiary, joined the tracks of the Southern on the west side of the main line just south of the passenger station.

Danville was also famous as the location of the wreck that inspired the popular ballad, "The Wreck of Old 97". On September 27, 1903, Southern Railway express mail train No. 97, with an engine, four postal cars and one express car, left the rails at a high rate of speed as it entered the curved trestle over the Stillhouse Branch in North Danville and plunged into the stream below. Eleven were killed and six injured in one of the worst train wrecks in Virginia history. However, memory of the train wreck has been kept alive not by the scope of the tragedy but by the ballad that was sung to the tune of an old folk song. The song became the first million selling record in the United States and continues to be performed to this day.

History also rode the rails of the Southern's Richmond Division. The line was built by the historic 140-mile Richmond and Danville Railroad that was chartered in 1848. The line was completed to the coal mines at Midlothian in 1850; Jetersville in 1851; Drakes Branch in 1853; and, finally to Danville in 1856. Throughout the War Between the States it served as an essential transportation link between Richmond and the rest of the Confederacy. With the fall of Richmond in 1865, President Jefferson Davis and the Confederate government fled the city for Danville over the rails of the R&D RR. The ravages of war left the R&D in deplorable condition and to acquire the capital needed to rebuild the line, its control was lost in 1871 to northern investors. What followed was an amazing story in the history of southern railroads as the little railroad that had served as a lifeline of the Confederacy became the cornerstone of a vast railroad empire that was being assembled by the Pennsylvania Railroad.

This is a view of the Dundee engine house and yard that was located just north of the Dan River at Danville on October 27, 1946. Southern's shop craft employees at Dundee serviced the Southern steam locomotives that operated into Danville over the Danville Division (Monroe to Danville), the Richmond Division (Richmond to Danville) and over the Norfolk Division (from Norfolk to Danville during the lease of the A&D). Class Ks 2-8-0 No. 850 is shown along with a number of locomotives of various classes and wheel arrangements. (David Driscoll Photo/William E. Griffin, Jr. Collection)

In 1873, the R&D was connected in Richmond with the line of the Richmond and York River Railroad. This railroad had been incorporated in 1853 and was completed in March of 1861 between Richmond and West Point on the York River (39 miles) to serve as a rail-steamboat route to Hampton Roads and Baltimore. Unfortunately, the railroad was opened less than a month before the Commonwealth of Virginia seceded from the union and it immediately played a role in military operations during the war. In 1862 and again in 1863 it was used by the Federal army as it advanced up the Peninsula to attack Richmond. In 1873, the line was reorganized as the Richmond, York River and Chesapeake Railroad and in 1880, the R&D and the RYR&C were merged to form the Richmond & West Point Terminal Railway & Warehouse Company. In the 1880's, the northern management of the line used this holding company to form a rail empire that accounted for nearly a third of all southern rail mileage and led in 1894 to the creation of the Southern Railway.

Another Southern Railway line that extended from the former R&D was the Richmond and Mecklenburg Railroad that was incorporated in 1875 to build a 31-mile railroad from Keysville, on the R&D, via Chase City to the town of Clarksville. It was opened for operation in 1884 and leased to the R&D in 1888, then acquired by the Southern in 1898. This line was extended into North Carolina by the Clarksville and North Carolina Railroad, which was also acquired by the Southern in 1894.

The lines of the Southern even reached into the coal fields of southwest Virginia. This was the Southern's Appalachia Division that extended west from Bristol to connect with the Clinchfield at Moccasin Gap and with the N&W, L&N and Interstate at Appalachia. The line was originally built by the Virginia and Southwestern Railway that was organized in 1896 to acquire two railroads that had been sold at a foreclosure sale. The Virginia and Southwestern was a single track line that operated solely in Tennessee and Virginia and operated a total of 207 miles when acquired by the Southern Railway in 1916. Its line extended into Tennessee from St. Charles and Moccasin Gap in Virginia with a branch line in the Commonwealth that extended from Big Stone Gap to Linden Mines. The historic Natural Tunnel that was carved by Stock Creek of the Clinch River was located on the line that extended in a southeasterly direction from St. Charles. The tunnel was a tourist stop for passenger trains of the V&SW RY and was used by freight trains operated by the Southern.

The final line operated by the Southern into the Commonwealth was owned by the ACL RR and used by the Southern pursuant to a trackage rights arrangement. Since 1883 the R&D RY had used West Point as its deep water terminal. However, the new Southern determined that a better terminal could be established at Pinners Point, opposite Norfolk on the Elizabeth River. The Southern was able to access Norfolk

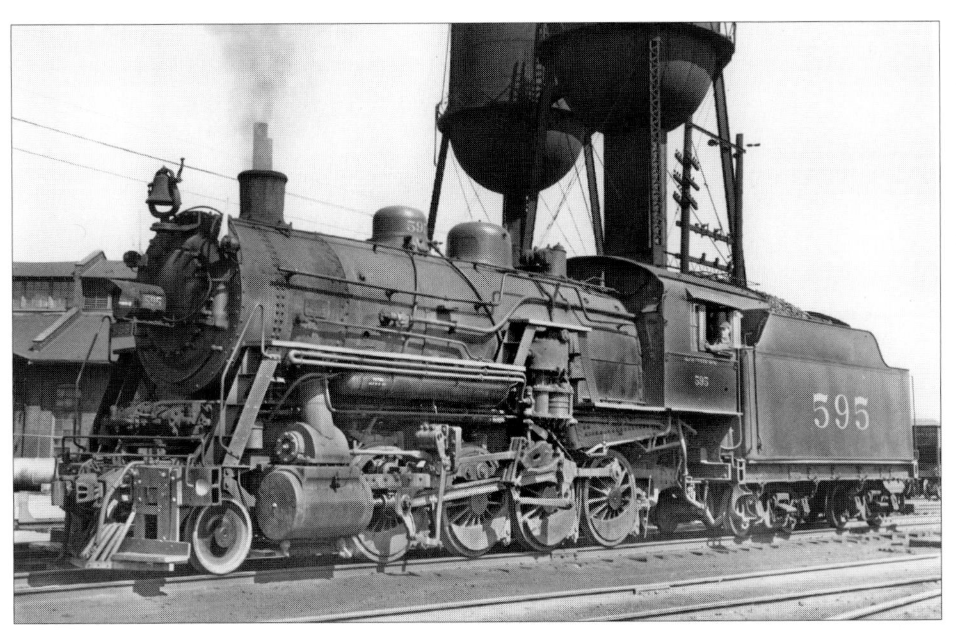

The Southern's yard at Monroe was the dividing point for the railroad's Washington and Danville divisions and was the away-from-home terminal for crews of both divisions. Locomotives received running repairs and maintenance for their outbound trips. Ks class 2-8-0 No. 595 is shown after servicing at the Monroe engine terminal on April 16, 1950. The Southern operated an extensive roster of Consolidation, or 2-8-0, type steam locomotives in the G, I, J and K classes. The K class locomotive, which would become the Southern's standard main line Consolidation type locomotive, was designed by the railroad's motive power department, working with representatives of both Baldwin and Richmond Locomotive Works. Eventually, the railroad and its affiliates would own over 400 of this class of locomotive. (Bob's Photo/William E. Griffin, Jr. Collection)

in 1896 by leasing one North Carolina railroad and obtaining trackage rights over two lines that were predecessor companies of the ACL RR. These arrangements extended the Southern's operations from Selma, North Carolina over the ACL line via Tarboro, North Carolina into Pinners Point. The Southern abandoned West Point as its principal deep water terminal and acquired property at Pinners Point where it built yards, wharves, docks and warehouses.

In 1980 the Southern Railway merged with the Norfolk and Western Railway to form the new Norfolk Southern Corporation, with its headquarters in Norfolk, and has retained its substantial presence in the Commonwealth of Virginia.

The Southern was one of the first railroads to dieselize its motive power and by the late 1940's diesels were used throughout the system. Southern class E6A No. 2800 is shown at the Washington Terminal Ivy City locomotive terminal on March 1, 1947. The slant nosed E6A's were delivered by EMD in May of 1941 to power two of the Southern's new stainless steel streamliners, the Southerner *and the* Tennessean. *Note that the 2800 has been lettered the* Southerner *for assignment to that train. The Southern ordered seven E6A's and four E6B's for these trains and they were delivered in the green, gold and white paint scheme with the name of the train to be handled lettered on both sides of the diesel locomotive. (William E. Griffin, Jr. Collection)*

From Manassas, the Southern Railway's Harrisonburg Branch ran westward across rolling meadows then ascended the eastern face of the Blue Ridge, crossed the Shenandoah River and wound through the Shenandoah Valley to Harrisonburg. Simply known as "The Branch" or "The Weed Line" to Southern railroaders, it was a single track line through terrain that was "just wild enough to be interesting". Until the automobile cut into its passenger service, the consist for Washington-Harrisonburg passenger trains could include an RPO, an express car, a combination smoker car, coach and a Pullman buffet parlor car. The operation of steam locomotives on the branch ended approximately at the same time as the discontinuance of passenger service. The last passenger trains were operated in 1948. Class Ps-2 Pacific No. 1348 is shown with a typical Harrisonburg Branch passenger train at Strasburg Junction. (John Krause Photo/William E. Griffin, Jr. Collection)

Southern Railway Train No. 11 departs Front Royal after a station stop in July 3, 1938. Front Royal is the county seat of Warren County and the line of the Harrisonburg does not go directly through the town. The main line was located at Front Royal Junction at Mile Post 82.5 with a spur line of approximately one mile into the town. (W. H. Thrall, Jr. Photo/Frank E. Ardrey, Jr. Collection)

The Southern Railway's 38-mile line from Richmond to West Point was built by the Richmond and York River Railroad initially for the purpose creating a rail and steamboat route to Hampton Roads and Baltimore. When the Southern Railway decided to abandon West Point as a deep water terminal in favor of Pinners Point at Portsmouth, the West Point line was used primarily as a freight line. In a classic view, Ks class 2-8-0 No. 880 is shown passing through the drawbridge at Great Ship Lock Park as it departs Richmond for its run to West Point. (J. I. Kelly Photo/William E. Griffn, Jr. Collection)

The Southern Railway's 14th Street Station in Richmond was built in 1900. Constructed of brick and granite, it had a tall square tower facing Main Street and was built at the southwest corner of 14th and Mill (Canal) streets. It was two and one half stories high with a gabled roof and a long covered platform on the west side with stub end station tracks. The station served the Southern passenger trains that operated to both Danville and West Point. The last passenger train left the station on March 14, 1914 as the station was razed to make way for a new freight station. (Russell Wayne Davis Collection)

The 14th Street Station in Richmond was replaced in 1915 by the Southern's new station in South Richmond on Hull Street. It was a one and one half story brick structure with a red tile roof served by one through station track, one passing track and two stub end set-out tracks. A covered platform adjoined the station track. This station was closed after the discontinuance of passenger service between Richmond and Danville effective February 16, 1957. In 1982, the station building was donated by the railroad to the Old Dominion Chapter, National Railway Historical Society and today it serves as the chapter's railroad museum. Here we see Ps-2 Pacific No. 1358 set to depart Hull Street Station in 1949 with Train No. 7. (D. Wallace Johnson Photo/William E. Griffin, Jr. Collection)

Departing the city of Richmond, the tracks of the Richmond Division snaked along the bank on the south side of the James River. Here we see a Southern Railway passenger train for Danville circa 1920 as it is about to pass under the James River Bridge of the ACL-RF&P James River Branch. (William E. Griffin, Jr. Collection)

This lineup of steam locomotives at the Pinners Point engine terminal includes J Class 2-8-0 No. 444 that is flying white flags and set to depart with a doublehead extra freight in 1947. (H. Reid Photo/ William E. Griffin, Jr. Collection)

Following its entry into the Norfolk area in the 1890's, the Southern built a substantial terminal at Pinners Point on the Portsmouth side of the Elizabeth River. To bridge the mile and a quarter of river between its freight houses at Norfolk and Pinners Point, the Southern conducted a naval operation consisting of a tugboat, an open barge, four car floats, fourteen house barges and a floating pile driver. This aerial view of the Pinners Point terminal, taken in 1959, shows the Southern Railway rail yard and piers to the left and the rail yard and piers of the ACL to the right. (Tal Carey Collection)

The Southern reached Pinners Point as a result of trackage rights granted by the ACL RR. In this view Southern Alco RS-3 diesel No. 6232 is shown on ACL tracks crossing the West Norfolk Branch of the Atlantic and Danville Railway at Boone Tower on May 11, 1962. The train has departed Pinners Point and will operate over the ACL until it rejoins Southern tracks at Selma, North Carolina. (Ralph Coleman Photo)

The Virginian Railway was unique among American railroad companies. Typically, American railroads were formed from groups of smaller roads that were then joined together by merger and acquisition to create the resultant railroad system. It was also the practice to route lines to intentionally reach populous areas where the railroad could generate the most passenger traffic. Railroads were also built on a piecemeal basis with construction dependent upon the company's ability to generate revenue or obtain financing. Stock had to be sold or bonds floated. As a result the railroads were often built in the most economical manner which later would lead to operational problems and the need to upgrade lines as business increased.

None of these characteristics of early railroads applied to the Virginian Railway. The VGN was one of the last Class I railroads to be built in the eastern Unites States and its was conceived and constructed through the efforts of one man: Henry Huddleston Rogers, a New York financier and industrialist. Rogers had amassed a fortune as an executive of John D. Rockefeller's Standard Oil Company and as a result of his own investments in various coal, oil, and railroad companies, becomming one of wealthiest men in the world. Since the VGN was built with Rogers' private resources, there was no need to sell stock, float bonds of seek state or county subscriptions. It was a railroad that began business with all new infrastructure and no debt.

Rogers' railroad was formed for one purpose: the transportation of bituminous coal from the southern West Virginia coal fields to Tidewater at Hampton Roads at the lowest practicable cost per ton-mile. Directness of route was the primary consideration involved in the planning and construction of its line. The VGN would be a supercarrier functioning like a conveyor belt on rails. To design and build his railroad, Rogers entered into a partnership with William Nelson Page, a Virginia civil engineer and entrepreneur who had assisted with the construction of the Chesapeake and Ohio Railway's double track in the New River and Kanawha River valleys. He was also a keen businessman who was aware of the potential for the transporation of the untapped bituminous coal fields in West Virginia. Given Rogers' deep pockets, cost of construction would not be a consideration. Natural barriers would be conquered by revolutionary techniques as well as the most generally approved standards and principles of construction known to railroad builders. Greater attention would be given to grades and alignment than had ever been considered in the building of a railroad. From Princeton, West Virginia to Tidewater Virginia, the VGN had no grade against the eastbound load exceeding 0.2 per cent, except for 9.4 miles of 0.6 per cent grade ascending the

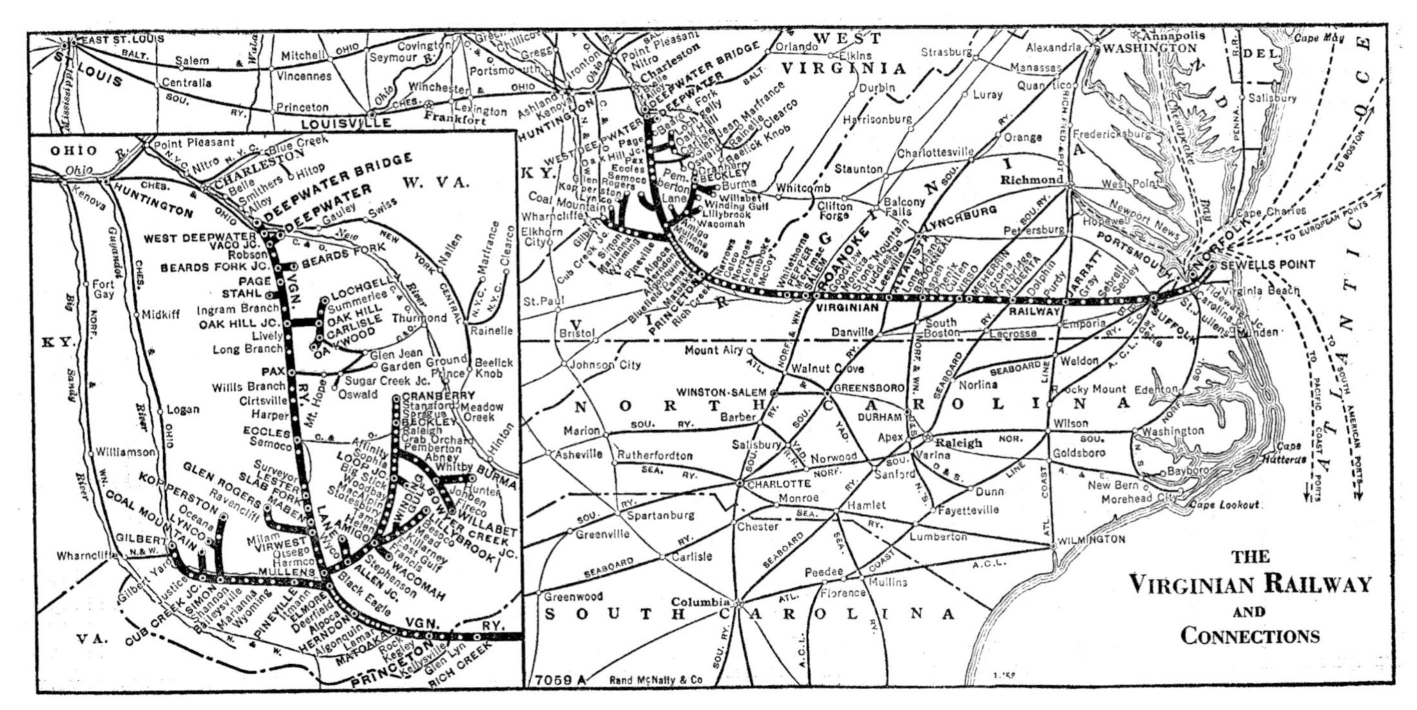

Allegheny Mountains. The road bed was laid with 130-pound rails and its structures were designed for heavy rolling stock and steam locomotives that included some of the largest in the world.

Rogers began construction of the VGN by acquiring the Deepwater Railway Company in 1902. The Deepwater had been incorporated under the general laws of West Virginia on January 25, 1898 and had purchased four miles of railroad from the Loop Creek Estate that was operating between Deepwater and Robson, West Virginia. In 1904, Rogers and his associates incorporated the Tidewater Railway Company and began construction of the railroad in the Commonwealth of Virginia. The work of establishing the right-of-way in Virginia began in February, 1904 and by February, 1906 the entire length of the railroad was under contract. The first track laid in Virginia was put down in 1905 near Algren and one of the first sections laid was between Brookneal and Roanoke.

By charter amendment on March 8, 1907, the name of the Tidewater Railway was changed to become the Virginian Railway. On April 22, 1907, the property and franchises of the Deepwater Railway were sold to the VGN. At the time of the VGN's purchase of the Deepwater Railway, the remaining 107 miles between Robson and the West Virginia-Virginia line were under construction. In 1907, Rogers also incorporated the Virginian Terminal Railway in Virginia for the purpose of acquiring a large tract of land at Sewalls Point and constructing a coal pier and other terminal facilities. The pier, yard tracks and other facilities were constructed at Sewalls Point between May, 1907 and July 1,1909 at which time the through line was placed in operation. [1]

As constructed, the VGN operated 657 miles of road, of which 333 miles were located in the Commonwealth of Virginia. Its main line extended from Sewalls Point (Norfolk), Virginia for 442 miles in a northwesterly direction, passing through the bituminous coal fields of southern West Virginia to Deepwater. A branch line of 44 miles in length extended from Elmore, West Virginia westerly along the Guyandotte River to Gilbert, West Virginia where connection was made with the Chesapeake and Ohio Railway and the Norfolk and Western Railway. Fourteen other branch lines, aggregating 107 miles, extended from connections with the main line and certain branch lines and served tributary areas of the southern West Virginia coal fields. The VGN entered the Commonwealth of Virginia from the west through the New River valley, crossed the Allegheny divide, followed the valley of the Roanoke River to Brookneal, traversed Southside Virginia and terminated at Norfolk. There were ten miles of double-track main line and 184 miles of sidings and industrial tracks in Virginia.

The VGN's primary yards in Virginia were located at Norfolk (Sewalls Point), Victoria and Roanoke. In fact, the town of Victoria was built to serve as the VGN's division point. Located approximately half way between Norfolk and Roanoke, it was also home terminal for East End road engineer and train crews. In addition to the yard, engine terminal with turntable, and 13-stall

[1]There are various spellings of the word "Sewalls". In this book we will use the spelling of the word as found in the VGN's employee timetable, i.e, "Sewalls Point".

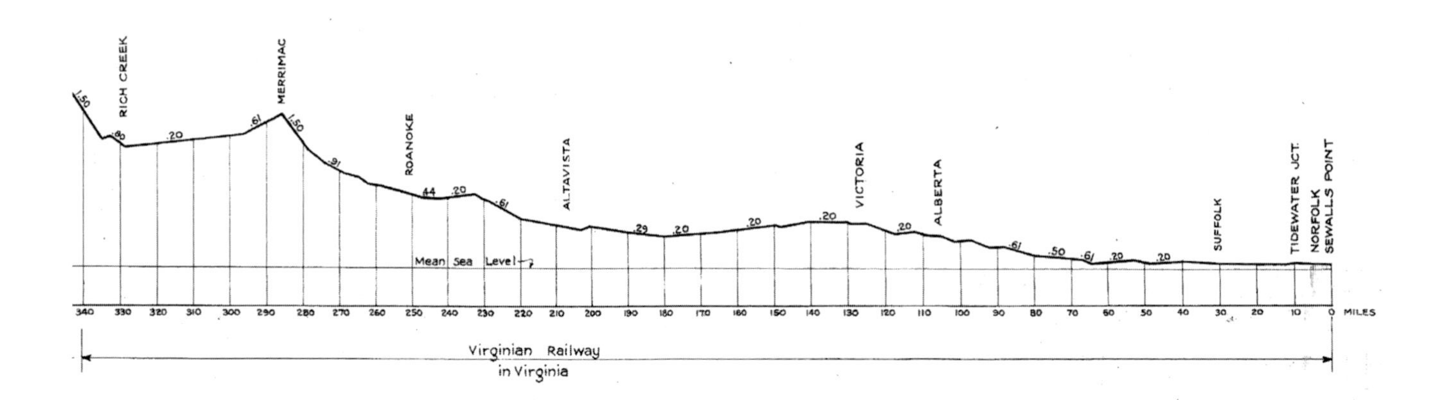

In 1907 the Virginian Terminal Railway was incorporated in Virginia to acquire and operate the coal pier and terminal facilities to be built at Sewalls Point in Norfolk. The pier, yard tracks and other facilities were built between May, 1907 and July 1, 1909 at which time through line service was placed in operation. Coal Pier No. 1 had cable-operated barneys that shoved a loaded coal car up an incline to a rotary dumper. Coal was originally dumped into electric conveyor cars that were barneyed to the top of the pier moving under their own power to chutes for discharge into the vessels below. Coal Pier No. 1 was rebuilt in 1939 to eliminate the numerous chutes with a loading tower. Pier No. 2 was built south of Pier No. 1 in 1925. Both piers were upgraded for electrical operation and were equipped to allay coal dust in the dumping process. This 1950's era view shows both piers, the Virginian tugboat W. R. Coe, and the yard facilities at Sewalls Point. (Dave George Collection)

roundhouse, a two story passenger station which also housed the division offices and East End train dispatchers were located at Victoria. The yard at Victoria primarily served as a staging yard to arrange for the shipments of coal to Norfolk.

At Sewalls Point, the VGN built special facilities for the handling of the coal shipped to Norfolk. The coal terminal consisted of two electrically operated piers to transfer coal from the railroad cars to ships. Pier No. 1 had a capacity of 5,400 tons per hour and provided sufficient space for two large vessels to load on each side at the same time. It was also a low level type pier that allowed coal to be placed in the ships with minimum breakage. In 1925, the VGN added a second pier (Pier No. 2) which had a capacity of 7,200 tons per hour. Four small vessels could be loaded simultaneously at this pier. Both of the Sewalls Point piers were equipped with "Sealtite Dedusters" that allayed coal dust in the dumping process.

In addition to the coal terminal, the Virgnian had a small locomotive termial at Sewells Point. This terminal had a five-stall roundhouse and was originally equipped with a 80-foot turntable, replaced in 1945 with a 130-foot table to accommodate the new AG class 2-6-6-6 type steam locomotives. Trip servicing and running repairs were performed here, but all major repairs and maintenance work for Virginian steam locomotives was performed at Princeton, West Virginia.

VGN operations east of Roanoke in Virginia were governed by the Norfolk Division which was headquarted at Victoria. The Norfolk Division was divided into the First Sub-Division (Sewalls Point to Victoria) and the Second Sub-Divsion (Victoria to Roanoke). The operating characteristics on the First and Second Sub-Divisions were similar. The maximum grades were .2 per cent eastbound and .6 per cent westbound. Prior to the acquisition of modern Lima-built steam power in the late 1940's, the principal locomotives in these districts were 2-8-8-2 mallet steam locomotives with tractive power of 110,200 pounds. These locomotives could handle 13,500 tons (165 loaded cars) eastbound, and 4,200 tons (about 165 empties) westbound. Passing tracks, yard tracks and other facilities were designed for this operation.

VGN operations west of Roanoke in Virginia were governed by the New River Division which was headquartered at Princeton, West Virginia in a building similar to the division office at Victoria. The New River Division was divided into the Third Sub-Divison (Roanoke to Elmore, West Virginia) and the Fourth Sub-Division (Elmore to D. B. Tower - Deepwater, West Virginia). The ruling grades between Roanoke and Elmore were 2.07 per cent for 14 miles eastbound between Elmore and Algonquin, West Virginia; .6 per cent for 9 miles eastbound between Whitethorne, Virginia and Merrimac, Virginia; 1.5 per cent for 7 miles westbound between Ellett, Virginia and Merrimac; and 1.5 per cent for 11 miles between Kelleysville, West Virginia and just east of Princeton. In 1926, the VGN electrified the 134 mile line between Mullens, West Virginia and Roanoke. Prior to electrification, the 2.07 per cent ruling grade eastbound between Elmore and Clarks Gap (just east of Algonquin) had required three steam locomotives to pull tonnage over the mountains. After electrification, two electric units moved even greater tonnage with comparative ease. Eastbound from Elmore, 6,000 ton freight trains were operated with two electric locomotives, one primary and one helper. From Clarks Gap to Roanoke, one electric locomotive handled 9,000 tons or about 110 cars loaded with coal. Westbound from Roanoke to Elmore, 3,000 tons (about 140 empty coal cars) were handled with one electric locomotive. The use of the electric motor as a regenerator on the down grade saved electric energy and enabled the train to maintain a constant speed without the use of brakes. The VGN built its own power plant at Narrows, Virginia to provide energy for its electrical operations.

In West Virginia the New River coal field was served principally by the C&O, the Winding Gulf field principally by the VGN, and the Pocahontas field by the N&W. The coal fields served by the VGN were in the center of the coal territory served by the C&O. Prior to the First World War, coal traffic represented about 90 per cent of the tonnage handled by the VGN. Practically all of the coal produced on its lines moved east. That situation changed in June, 1925, when joint rates westbound were established with the N&W via Matoaka and by October of that year the westbound movement of VGN coal via that junction totaled over 200,000 tons. Then in 1930, a new trunk line route between East and West was cre-

VGN MB class 2-8-2's Nos. 459 and 432 are receiving between trip servicing in the Sewalls Point roundhouse. (H. Reid Photo/Tal Carey Collection)

ated when the VGN and the Kanawha & Michigan Railway (New York Central System) opened a new bridge spanning the Kanawha River at Deepwater, West Virginia. This link connected the VGN with the Ohio Central lines of the NYC, a non-competing line, and gave the VGN a short line outlet to the West. After 1930 the VGN was able to share with other carriers the through traffic of the Midwestern states moving to and from the ports of Hampton Roads. This enabled the VGN to diversify its operations by hauling commodities other than coal. The VGN handled this business with fast time freights that operated daily between Norfolk and the New York Central's yard at Dickinson, West Virginia. The VGN's time freight service to and from the west connected with the ACL at Jarratt, Virginia; the SAL at Alberta, Virginia, the Southern Railway for westbound traffic at Virso, Virginia and with the Southern Railway at Altavista, Virginia for eastbound traffic. At Suffolk, Virginia, the VGN made freight connections with the ACL, N&W, SAL and Southern (A&D). At Norfolk, the VGN made freight connections with ACL, C&O, Pennsylvania, SAL and Southern (A&D) via the Norfolk and Portsmouth Belt Line Railroad. It also connnected with the Norfolk Southern in Norfolk at Carolina Junction and Tidewater Junction.

While the VGN was designed to haul coal it also offered a modest passenger service in the Commonwealth of Virginia with daily passenger trains in both directions between Norfolk and Roanoke. Westbound No. 3 departed Norfolk Terminal Station at 8 AM with a scheduled arrival time of 4 PM in Roanoke. Eastbound No. 4 departed Roanoke at 8 AM with a scheduled arrival time in Norfolk of 4 PM. The trains arranged meeting point was Nutbush, just west of Victoria. On the west end, the VGN operated Nos. 3 and 4 daily between Roanoke and Deepwater as well as a number of locals and mixed trains to serve the coal branch lines. However, all of the locals and mixed trains were gone by the end of the 1930's. In 1954, the Virginia State Corporation Commission gave the VGN permission to discontinue all passenger service in Virginia west of Roanoke. The SCC denied the VGN's 1954 petition to discontinue its passenger service east of Roanoke based on a finding that the railroad operated its passenger service without regard to the needs of the communities and with no thought of encouraging passenger traffic. It ordered the VGN to provide an improved service for a period of not less than 12 months with better equipment and if there was still no substantial improvement in the ridership of the trains, then the Commission would reconsider the petition for discontinuance of service. To comply with the SCC's order, the VGN began to operate air-conditioned coaches leased from the N&W on its trains between Norfolk and Roanoke. However, ridership of the trains did not improve and on November 1, 1955, the VGN's contract with the US Post Office Department was cancelled. The VGN promptly refiled with the SCC to discontinue the trains and this time the railroad's petition was approved. The last runs of passenger service over the VGN in Virginia occurred on January 29, 1956.

Throughout its history the VGN operated its trains with an interesting roster of steam, diesel and electric locomotives. Some of the VGN's largest articulated steam locomotives, such as the Baldwin Triplex Mallet 2-8-8-8-4 built for pusher service on the Clark's Gap grade, worked exclusively in West Virginia. However, the AE class 2-10-10-2 mallets did work between Princeton and Roanoke and, after 1925, were assigned to coal trains between Roanoke and Victoria. Until 1945, the steam locomotives primarily assigned to coal trains on the east end were the 700-series US class 2-8-8-2 locomotives. The VGN owned four classes of Mikado steam locomotives and the MB class 2-8-2's could handle 80-car coal trains from Roanoke to Victoria and 100-car trains from Victoria to Sewalls Point. They could also be found on mine runs and local freights. Dur-

AG class 2-6-6-6 type steam locomotives Nos. 907 and 906 are being serviced at Sewalls Point on February 28, 1953. These Lima built locomotives in the number series 900-907 were delivered to the Virginian in 1945 to handle 165-car coal trains between Roanoke and Sewalls Point. Known as the Blue Ridge type on the Virginian, they were almost identical to the H-8 class locomotives built by Lima for the C&O. They were single cycle articulated locomotives with cast steel bed frames and integral cylinders. Fully loaded, the AG class held 25 tons of coal and 26,500 gallons of water. They had 67-inch drivers, weighed 753,000 pounds and were rated at 110,200 pounds of tractive effort. (H. Reid Photo/Tal Carey Collection)

ing its final years of steam operation, the VGN introduced two modern steam locomotives to its freight locomotive roster. In 1945, the VGN purchased eight giant Allegheny class 2-6-6-6 type, single-expansion articulated locomotives from Lima that could handle trains of 14,500 tons (165 cars) over the eastern half of the road. Numbered in the 900-907 series they were virtually identical to the C&O H-8 class 2-6-6-6 type locomotives. Then in 1946, the VGN acquired fast freight Berkshire 2-8-4 type locomotives (Nos. 500-509) from Lima that were similar to the C&O K-4 2-8-4 type locomotives. They were assigned to Time Freights Nos. 71-72 and 73-74. The VGN also upgraded its switchers when it acquired second hand 1942-1943 Lima-built 0-8-0's from the C&O in 1950. Modern steam power never was assigned to the VGN passenger trains. These trains were handled by 4-4-0 and 4-6-0 type locomotives until all-steel equipment was adopted for the passenger trains. Beginning in 1920, the main line trains were assigned to the PA class 4-6-2's in the number series 210-215. These locomotives would handle the main line passenger trains until the end of that service on the railroad.

The VGN dieselized its locomotive roster between 1954 and 1957 with a fleet of sixty-five diesels from Fairbanks Morse. Forty diesels in the number series 10-49 were 1,600-horsepower Class DE-S B-B type units that produced a tractive effort of 65,500 pounds. Twenty-five diesels in the number series 50-74 were 2,400-horsepower Class DE-RS C-C Trainmaster type units that produced a tractice effort of 98,625 pounds. The twenty-five Trainmasters were primarily used on the west end, west of Clarks Gap and on yard assignments at Elmore. The forty-five 1,600-horsepower units worked the east end, replacing the 2-8-4's and 2-6-6-6's on road assignments between Roanoke and Sewalls Point. The only other diesel owned by the VGN was General Electric 44-ton switcher No. 6 that was used for industrial and interchange switching at Suffolk. Electric locomotives used on the electrified district between Mullens, West Virginia and Roanoke were initially boxcab type EL-3A units (the "Squareheads") from a variety of builders. In later years, assignments in this area were handled by General Electric EL-2B units (the "Steamliners") and the General Electric EL-C (the "Bricks").

When one considers the efficient and profitable nature of the VGN's operations and infrastructure it not surprising that the railroad was an early target for acquisition by the larger rail systems. During the takeover of the railroads by the USRA throughout the years of the First World War, the VGN was jointly operated with the N&W by the Director General of the railroads. After the war, there were numerous attempts by the larger roads to acquire the VGN. In the Interstate Commerce Commission's tentative plan for the consolidation of railroads, the VGN was grouped with the C&O system. Recognizing the efficiencies in their joint operation

The VGN dieselized its train operations on the east end beginning in 1954 with the delivery 1,600-horsepower 4-axle DE-S class diesel locomotives built by Fairbanks Morse. The VGN would own thirty-eight of these locomotives in the number series 10-49 delivered between 1954 and 1957. The number series included Nos. 48 and 49 that were purchased to replace Nos. 23 and 28 that were destroyed in a wreck. A group of the DE-S units, including Nos. 21, 40 and 38, are lined up at Sewalls Point. (Steve Gibson Collection)

during the war, the N&W quickly began negotiations to lease the VGN after the ICC's plan was made public. In 1924 a joint lease of the VGN by the C&O and N&W was proposed by the C&O's Van Sweringen interests but the proposal was rejected by the N&W. In 1926 the N&W submitted a proposal to the ICC to lease the VGN but that petition was rejected by the ICC based on opposition by the C&O, B&O, the Commonwealth of Virginia, the state of West Virginia and various business and community groups.

The N&W never lost sight of the inherent efficiencies in the joint operation of the two roads. The VGN and N&W were substantially parallel from Norfolk to Kelleysville, West Virginia. Between Norfolk and Roanoke they were at no point more than approximately thirty miles apart. From Roanoke west to Kelleysville they were not more than five miles apart at any point and were in sight of each other for a large part of the distance. In Virginia, the lines of the two railroads came in contact at Norfolk, Abilene, Valbrook, Roanoke, Salem, Merrimac and Norcross. Merger of the VGN and N&W was finally approved by the ICC effective December 1, 1959. While the identity of the VGN was lost in its merger with the N&W, the interest and fascination with the railroad continues with grow among railfans and historians with each passing year.

The workhorse of the VGN's fleet of steam locomotives for almost the entire history of the railroad was the MB class 2-8-2 type locomotives. The VGN owned 42 of these locomotives in the number series 420-461 that were built by Baldwin for the VGN in 1909 and 1910. From the date of their delivery until the end of steam operations, these locomotives handled every type of service demanded by the railroad. On the east end they could handle 80-car coal trains from Roanoke to Victoria and 100-car coal trains from Victoria to Sewalls Point. They could also be found on mine runs, work trains, time freights, locals, yard switchers and even passenger runs. With the delivery of the AG class 2-6-6-6's and BA class 2-8-4's in the late-1940's, the MB's ended their career on east end local freights. MB class 2-8-2 No. 448 nears Sewalls Point with a local freight in 1953. (H. Reid Photo/William E. Griffin, Jr. Collection)

The VGN gained access to downtown Norfolk via trackage rights over the Norfolk Southern. Between 1910 and 1912, the VGN, N&W and NS built a new downtown passenger terminal at Norfolk that also provided office space for the railroads and housed the VGN and NS general offices. VGN trains entered the NS tracks at Tidewater Junction where the double track line of the VGN crossed the single line of the NS. The NS line extended to the passenger station in Norfolk then eastward through Tidewater Junction to Virginia Beach where it connected to form a loop with the NS line that crossed the VGN at Coleman Place. The track layout at Tidewater Junction included an interchange connection so that passenger and local freight trains of the VGN were routed over the NS between Tidewater Junction and the passenger station as well as the VGN freight terminal in Norfolk. In this photo looking generally north, PA class 4-6-2 No. 214 with Train No. 4 is backing past Tidewater Junction tower and crossing over to the east main line tracks. (T. G. Wicker Photo/William E. Griffin, Jr. Collection)

Eastbound VGN passenger trains pulled into Norfolk Terminal passenger station after moving over the two miles of NS trackage. After unloading their passengers, mail and express, the trains then backed out of the terminal and were moved to Sewalls Point for servicing prior to the next day's trip. Conversely, westbound trains backed into the station over NS tracks from Tidewater Junction and then pulled out for their trip. PA class 4-6-2 No. 210 is prepared to depart the Norfolk Terminal Station with passenger train No. 3 in 1954 for its seven and one-half hour run to Roanoke. (Edward Patterson Photo/William E. Griffin, Jr. Collection)

The main waiting room of the Norfolk Terminal Passenger Station in 1930. The passenger station was located on the ground floor with eight floors of office space above the station. The Norfolk Southern occupied the second through the fourth floors, the VGN occupied floors five through seven and two top floors were occupied by the N&W. The general offices of the both the NS and VGN were located in their respective office space in the building. (Carlton Parker Photo/Herbert H. Harwood, Jr. Collection)

Prior to the VGN's acquisition of the PA class 4-6-2's, passenger trains were handled by the EA class 4-4-0's and the TA class 4-6-0's. The EA class locomotives were built for the VGN predecessor Deepwater Railway by Baldwin in 1906-07. These locomotives were not equipped with stokers and required constant manual attention by the locomotive firemen. This photo of EA class 4-4-0 No. 296 was taken in the early 1930's as the locomotive handled its passenger train to Sewalls Point after the station stop at the Norfolk Terminal Station. In providing information for this photo, which came from his collection, H. Reid exhibited his usual wonderful sense of humor. He said that the veteran VGN fireman denied that he was the engineman seated in the cab window of the photograph. "It couldn't be me in that picture", he said. "I never sat down in an EA". (H. T. Crittenden Photo/William E. Griffin, Jr. Collection from H. Reid)

Coleman Place interlocking was located 6.3 miles west of Sewalls Point where the double track main line of the VGN crossed the two main line tracks of the NS, one of those tracks being operated by the Pennsylvania Railroad under trackage rights with the NS. In the late-1940's Coleman Place was a busy interlocking. Six NS trains operated over its line. The Pennsylvania RR, which operated between St Julian Yard and the ferry slips on Little Creek, operated 18 daily transfer trains over the NS main line through Coleman Place. The VGN operated 25 to 30 trains daily through the interlocking and there were also numerous interchange movements. H. Reid stood on a signal mast to capture this cab level view of VGN MB class 2-8-2 No. 422 approaching the crossing at grade with the NS at Coleman Place interlocking on June, 1948. (H. Reid Photo/TLC Collection)

Prior to the arrival of the AG class 2-6-6-6, the coal trains between Roanoke and Sewalls Point were handled by MB class 2-8-2's and US class 2-8-8-2's in the 700 number series. The 700-series locomotives were USRA heavy Mallet compound steam locomotives, developed during the First World War. Here 2-8-8-2 No. 701 rolls a train of the VGN's "battleship gondola" cars through Carolina Junction on July 11, 1948. (Bob's Photo/William E. Griffin, Jr. Collection)

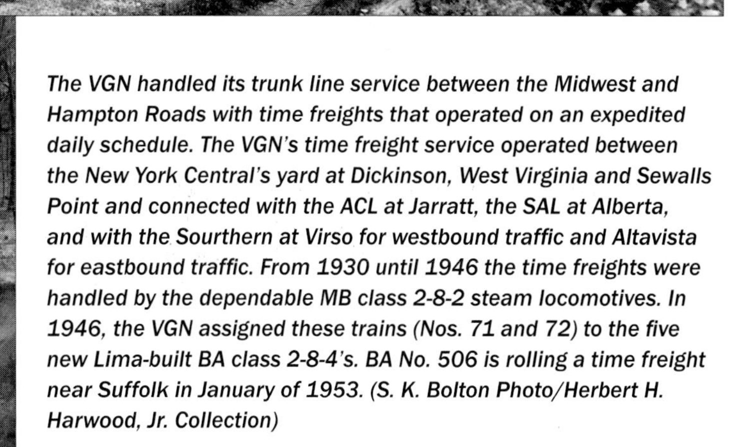

The VGN handled its trunk line service between the Midwest and Hampton Roads with time freights that operated on an expedited daily schedule. The VGN's time freight service operated between the New York Central's yard at Dickinson, West Virginia and Sewalls Point and connected with the ACL at Jarratt, the SAL at Alberta, and with the Sourthern at Virso for westbound traffic and Altavista for eastbound traffic. From 1930 until 1946 the time freights were handled by the dependable MB class 2-8-2 steam locomotives. In 1946, the VGN assigned these trains (Nos. 71 and 72) to the five new Lima-built BA class 2-8-4's. BA No. 506 is rolling a time freight near Suffolk in January of 1953. (S. K. Bolton Photo/Herbert H. Harwood, Jr. Collection)

In Suffolk, the VGN shared in the operation of the passenger station with the SAL. The Suffolk station, currently owned by the Suffolk-Nansemond Historical Society, was erected in 1885 and remodeled in 1920. Typical of stations built during the late 19th century, it featured bracketed eaves and a Queen Anne style tower. The tracks of the two railroads passed on opposite sides of the buildings. VGN eastbound passenger train No. 4 is pulling away on the remaining portion of its run to Norfolk after a stop at the distinctive Suffolk station. (Tal Carey Collection)

The VGN and the SAL operated largely on the north side of the town of Suffolk and initially they reached very few of the industries. In 1940, the NS sold its properties in Suffolk to VGN, which then gave the SAL trackage rights over the former NS trackage under a joint operating agreement so that terminal switching could be performed by either road. During the steam era, the VGN switching work at Suffolk was performed by SA class 0-8-0 switchers. When the VGN dieselized its motive power, the Suffolk switching duties were performed by second hand General Electric 44-ton switcher No. 6. The GE switcher had the distinction of being the only non-Fairbanks Morse diesel owned by the VGN. Here No. 6 is shown at Suffolk in 1954 shortly after its delivery to the VGN from its previous owner R. C. Stanhope, Inc. (Bob Lorenz Photo/Tal Carey Collection)

Located at Mile Post 73.7, Jarrett was an important point for the interchange of freight traffic between the VGN and the ACL. The main lines of the two railroads crossed at an interlocked grade crossing and interchange tracks connected the two lines. There was also an important 7620-foot passing siding at Jarrett that would hold a 190-car train. In this view we see VGN 2-8-4 No. 509 steaming through Jarrett with a time freight on June 1, 1953. (H. Reid Photo/ William E. Griffin, Jr. Collection)

Located midway between Norfolk and Roanoke, the town of Victoria was founded by the VGN to serve as the division headquarters for the east end of the railroad. Henry H. Rogers is credited with naming the town after Queen Victoria of England. A two-story station served as the passenger station, division headquarters and east end train dispatcher's office. There was a 13-stall (later 9 stalls) roundhouse, a turntable, steam locomotive shops and an 86-acre rail yard. This splendid view looking west on May 3, 1953 shows portions of the engine terminal on the left where an AG 2-6-6-6 is being serviced. A class SB 0-8-0 switcher is drifting past a cut of caboose cars and another cut of hopper cars stand in front of the combination passenger station/division office. The highway overpass at the west end of the yard provided an excellent vantage point to view and photograph the yard operations. (H. Reid Photo/TLC Collection)

VGN westbound passenger train No. 3 arrives at Victoria behind PA class 4-6-2 No. 215 on June 20, 1955 as DE-S diesel No. 29 waits in the yard. Even though the VGN began to remove steam locomotives from its freight operations, the steam locomotives would remain on its passenger trains until that service was discontinued in 1956. (Bob's Photo/William E. Griffin, Jr. Collection)

Meeting for the last time, VGN passenger trains Nos. 3 and 4 met at Victoria instead of their usual meeting point at Nutbush. Eastbound No. 3 was pulled by PA 4-6-2 No. 212 and PA 4-6-2 No. 213 handled westbound No. 4. Hundreds of people up and down the line waved at the last runs while others stood silent or sat in their automobiles, watching sadly. (H. Reid Photo/William E. Griffin, Jr. Collection)

Photographed from the highway overpass at the west end of the yard, Herbert Harwood captured this view of a pair of DE-S units (Nos. 20 and 39) departing Victoria with a west-bound hopper train in March of 1956. The town of Victoria and the passenger station are to the left in the photo. To the right is the yard and engine terminal. (Herbert H. Harwood, Jr. Photo)

The normal meeting point for the VGN passenger trains was at Nutbush (Mile Post 125.2) which was approximately 6 miles west of Victoria. In September, 1955, PA 4-6-2 No. 210 waits in the passing siding at Nutbush while PA 4-6-2 No. 214 recedes into the distance with No. 3. The scheduled meet time for the trains was 12:03 p.m. (H. Reid Photo/William E. Griffin, Jr. Collection)

Storming across the trestle at Mile Post 196, east of Altavista, AG 2-6-6-6 No. 900 rolls an Extra East on August 21, 1951. The AG's shook the earth when they stormed past with their 165-car coal trains providing a sight never to be forgotten by those who were fortunate enough to witness their passing. (H. Reid Photo/William E. Griffin, Jr. Collection)

VGN PA class 4-6-2 No. 412 accelerates eastbound passenger train No. 4 from the Roanoke passenger station. The train is passing under Walnut Avenue and across the crossing at grade with the N&W's Winston-Salem line. The building to the left of the train is JR Tower which controlled the interlocked crossing. Note that there is no catenary under the train as the VGN's electrified line ended at Walnut Avenue. Also note the sign hanging from the bridge above the locomotive's tender. This sign alerted traffic headed west under Walnut Avenue that the electrified territory began at that point. (TLC Collection)

This rare view of the Roanoke locomotive facilities was taken on August 23, 1951. Located at the foot of Mill Mountain, the facilities handled the servicing of steam, diesel and electric locomotives. (H. Reid Photo/TLC Collection)

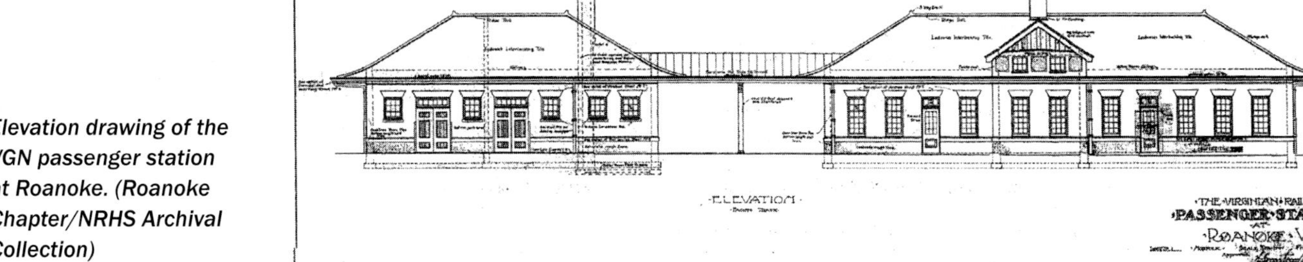

Elevation drawing of the VGN passenger station at Roanoke. (Roanoke Chapter/NRHS Archival Collection)

Looking across the VGN's yard at Roanoke in 1956 we see two loaded coal trains and three long cuts of empty hoppers. The DE-S diesel is working in yard service. Following the dieselization of its motive power, the VGN did not acquire yard switchers as was the case with other railroads. The VGN's 4-axle 1,600-horsepower Fairbanks-Morse diesels handled both yard and road service assignments. (C. K. Marsh, Jr. Photo/William E. Griffin, Jr. Collection)

With its typical consist, westbound passenger train No. 3 is making its stop at the Roanoke station in July of 1952. (Joseph Brauwer Photo/Herbert H. Harwood, Jr. Collection)

In this wonderful image by Richard J. Cook a set of EL-2B "streamliners" takes a loaded train of Virginian's famous high capacity gondoloa cars (the 100 ton "battleship" gons) East toward Roanoke and thence on to Tidewater. Bought in 1948, the massive 6,800 HP General Electric locomotives used a motor-generator set in each unit to step the 25 KV AC trolley current down to 600 V or so for the DC traction motors. Unlike the later EL-Cs, these units were not equipped with MU controls and thus not capable of operating with other locomotives. (Richard J. Cook photo, Allen County Historical Society Collection)

In October, 1956 the VGN began recieving 12 3,300 HP General Electric class EL-C electric locomotives, replacing at least some of the 1925 vintage EL-3A "squarehead" electrics. Unlike the earlier EL-3A and EL-2B locomotives, the EL-Cs used ignitron rectifiers to convert the AC current from the trolly wire to DC current, which was fed to DC traction motors identical to those used on contemporary Diesel locomotives. Also like contemporary Diesels, the EL-Cs were equipped with dynamic brakes, and could be operated with MU control in sets of up to four units. Here EL-Cs 138 and 139 rest at Roanoke, ready to return West with another string of empty coal cars. They will soon return with a similar train of loaded cars. (TLC Collection)

At Glen Lyn, the VGN crossed the New River on a high bridge that also spanned the main line of the N&W on the south side of the river. The river formed the boundary between the State of West Virginia and the Commonwealth of Virginia. In this view, PA class 4-6-2 No. 215 is crossing the state lines with eastbound Train No. 4 on the East River Bridge just west of Glen Lyn on August 26, 1951. (H. Reid Photo/TLC Collection)

The Atlantic Coast Line Railroad operated over 5,000 miles of road in the states of Virginia, North Carolina, South Carolina, Georgia, Florida, and Alabama. In the Commonwealth of Virginia it operated two separate important main lines of railroad. The primary route was the double track main line that was operated between Florida and Richmond. The other line branched off the double track main line at Rocky Mount, North Carolina and was operated via Tarboro, North Carolina and Suffolk, Virginia to Pinners Point.

The ACL's predecessor companies in the Commonwealth of Virginia were some of the earliest rail lines to be built in North America. The earliest predecessor was the Petersburg Railroad Company, chartered on February 10, 1830 to build a railroad from Petersburg, Virginia to "some convenient point on the North Carolina line." Construction of the line began in March, 1833 and was completed in August of that year to Blakely, a point just below the falls of the Roanoke River near Weldon, North Carolina. The earliest ACL predecessor company to reach Richmond, Virginia was the Richmond and Petersburg Railroad, chartered on March 14, 1838 to build a rail line between its namesake cities. Construction of the line began immediately and by May the 22 miles of its railroad had been completed between Richmond and Pocahontas on the north bank of the Appomattox River across from Petersburg. While these two ACL predecessor railroads had been built for the purpose of attracting trade to the cities that had obtained their charters and paid for their construction, they soon became important links in the route of transportation between the North and South.

During the War Between the States, the ACL predecessor rail lines (which had commonly come to be known as the "Weldon Route") were strategically located. After the fall of Norfolk, Wilmington, North Carolina became the major port serving the northern part of the Confederacy. The rail lines of the Weldon Route formed the main line of supply between Wilmington and the capitol of the Confederacy at Richmond and were constantly guarded by the Confederate Army until late in the conflict. However, with the fall of Richmond on April 3, 1865 the evacuating Confederate army

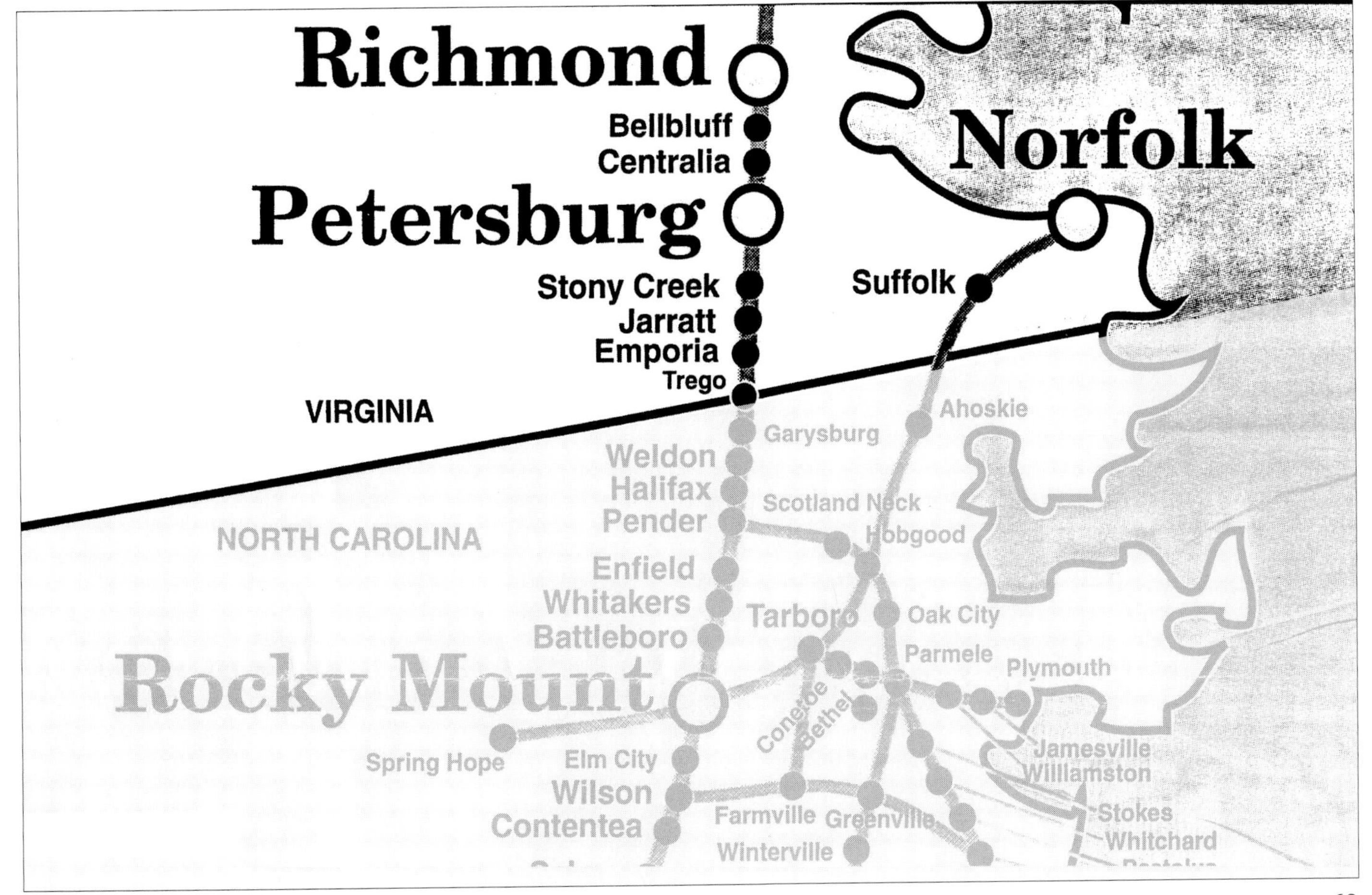

Due to the easy grades on its line between Richmond and Jacksonville, the ACL was unique in its operation of Pacific type 4-6-2 steam locomotives in both passenger and freight service, however, increasing equipment weights and train lengths required frequent doubleheading of these locomotives. Here ACL class P-5-B 4-6-2 No. 1672 and class P-5-A No. 1562 round the curve at Falling Creek in South Richmond with a southbound freight train in 1947. The train has just left the James River Branch and is headed south on the ACL main line passing FA Tower (behind the second locomotive) en-route to Petersburg. Construction of the James River Branch by the ACL and RF&P enabled the railroads to cease operation on the streets in Richmond and made the branch the ACL's primary route in and out of the city. (J. I. Kelly Photo/William E. Griffin, Jr. Collection)

burned the Richmond and Petersburg's bridge across the James River between Manchester and Richmond. The fire spread and also destroyed most of the railroad's shops, depot and offices.

After the war, Northern financiers gained control of the railroads and immediately set about the task of repairing the lines. Beginning in the 1870's, the railroads that comprised the Weldon Route began to be referred to as the "Atlantic Coast Line." It was a term adopted because the roads closely paralleled the Atlantic Ocean. Initially this term was merely used as the designation of a route and the component railroads retained their individual names. During the 1880's, Baltimore produce merchant William T. Walters and his banking associate, Benjamin F. Newcomer, acquired control of the "Atlantic Coast Line" railroads and the RF&P. With the RF&P and Weldon Route railroads firmly under his control, Walters implemented a number of new through freight and passenger operations over his evolving "Atlantic Coast Line" system of railroads. In 1888 the Walters system of railroads commenced operation of the *New York and Florida Special*, a Pullman passenger train that ran between New York and Jacksonville, Florida. Also in 1888, a new fast freight service known as the "Atlantic Coast Dispatch" was established for the movement of fresh fruits and vegetables in train loads from the South to northern markets. Both passenger and freight traffic dramatically increased over the system roads during this period.

To accommodate the steadily increasing traffic, the RF&P and Richmond and Petersburg Railroad built a new passenger station and train shed at the corner of Canal and 7th Streets in Richmond. Opened on April 10, 1887, the new Byrd Street Station also provided space for the general offices of the two railroads. Adjoining the new station was the freight terminal of the

Richmond and Petersburg Railroad and a yard for receipt and delivery of RF&P carload freight. Business was booming for both the RF&P and the Richmond and Petersburg but the increased traffic precipitated a controversy with the City of Richmond, which passed an ordinance prohibiting the use of steam locomotives on the city streets after April 8, 1890. While the railroads denied the legality of the ordinance (which was never enforced by the city), a belt line was built around Richmond, removing freight trains from congested city streets. The belt line, which would come to be known as the "James River Branch", would skirt to the northwest of the Richmond city limit and to the west and south of the corporate limit of Manchester. The branch would include a substantial new steel bridge over the James River. This bridge paid for and owned by the RF&P and the Richmond and Petersburg Railroad, with the former owning the 3.34 miles north of the center of the bridge (Pier 5) and the later owning the 4.54 miles south of that point. Construction of the branch began in 1888 and it was opened, for freight service only, on February 2, 1891. Pursuant to contract, the entire branch was operated by the RF&P for the joint account of the RF&P and the Richmond and Petersburg Railroad. Through passenger service continued to be provided at Byrd Street Station.

It was during this period that the ACL also established the operation into Virginia of its second main line, to the Norfolk area. The Walters syndicate desired to participate in the commercial shipping at the growing harbor of Hampton Roads. In 1886, they acquired the Western Branch Railway that had been chartered to build a rail line from Pinners Point on the Western Branch of the Elizabeth River to Drivers in Nansemond County near the town of Suffolk. Another ACL predecessor company, the Chowan and Southern Railroad was chartered to build a rail line between Drivers and Tarboro, North Carolina. In 1888, the Western Branch Railway was absorbed into the Chowan and Southern, which was renamed the Norfolk and Carolina Railroad in 1889. This 100-mile line from Pinners Point to Tarboro was completed in 1890. At Tarboro, the Norfolk and Carolina RR joined an extension of another ACL predecessor, the Wilmington and Weldon Railroad, which had been built between Rocky Mount and Tarboro in 1860.

When the James River Branch was doubletracked in 1918, a new monumental concrete arch bridge that was designed by J. E. Greiner was built over the James River. In addition to the doubletracking of the branch and construction of the new bridge, the tracks north of the river were depressed below ground level to eliminate grade crossings, and concrete bridges over these tracks were built at Broad Street, Monument Avenue, Patterson Avenue and Grove Avenue. The ACL operated over the RF&P's portion of the branch from Pier 5 of the James River Bridge to Acca Yard for freight service and to Broad Street Station for passenger service. An ACL Pacific (4-6-2) is shown crossing the new double track James River Bridge with a northbound freight headed for Acca Yard. (ACL Photo/TLC Collection)

The ACL also built a belt line around the city of Petersburg to eliminate operation over the downtown streets. Built in 1895, the belt line was constructed west of the city and ran from north of Collier Yard to Dunlop. The southern junction of the belt line and the old main line to downtown Petersburg was located at "BX" Tower. H. Reid captured this classic view as the engine crew on one of the ACL's 4-6-2's slows to pick up orders for their southbound extra from the operator at "BX" Tower in the late 1940's. (H. Reid Photo/ William E. Griffin, Jr. Collection)

By 1890, the Walters syndicate had established important main lines to both Richmond and Norfolk in the Commonwealth of Virginia and it was decided that the time had come to simplify the corporate structure of their rail system. On November 21, 1898 the Virginia legislature authorized the merger of the Petersburg Railroad into the Richmond and Petersburg Railroad with the new company to be known as the "Atlantic Coast Line Railroad Company of Virginia." That same year, the South Carolina legislature approved the consolidation of the five Walters railroads operating between Wilmington, North Carolina and Columbia and Charleston, South Carolina as a new corporation to be known as the "Atlantic Coast Line Railroad Company of South Carolina." On April 21, 1900, the ACL RR of South Carolina, along with the Wilmington and Weldon and other railroads were merged into the ACL RR of Virginia, which then changed its name to the Atlantic Coast Line Railroad Company. In 1902 the Plant System of railroads was acquired by the ACL giving the company substantially the form of corporate structure that would exist until 1967.

In 1916 the ACL and RF&P jointly agreed to rebuild and double track the James River Branch and to build a new passenger station that would be operated in the interest of both railroads by a jointly owned terminal company. Under the agreement the two railroads chartered the Richmond Terminal Railway Company to erect and operate the new station. The magnificent new station was opened for service at noon on January 6, 1919. The track layout at Broad Street Station was unique. The tracks formed a loop so that both northbound and southbound trains of the ACL and RF&P operated through the station in the same direction. Northbound trains of the ACL approached the station over the James River Branch and the south leg of the Acca wye, entering the station from the west. All trains departed the station from the east, passing around the loop. Broad Street Station would serve as the passenger terminal for both the ACL (later SCL) and the RF&P until the assumption of intercity passenger service by the National Railroad Passenger Corporation (Amtrak) in 1971. ACL and Norfolk and Western Railway joint operation of through passenger trains that provided service between Richmond and Norfolk via Petersburg also shifted to operation over the James River Branch to Broad Street Station in 1919, vacating Byrd Street Station.

Concurrent with the construction of Broad Street Station, the RF&P began the work of double-tracking and depressing the tracks on the

James River Branch. The new branch included a monumental concrete arch bridge over the James River. The tracks north of the James River were depressed below ground level to eliminate grade crossings, which involved the construction of four massive overhead concrete bridges for Broad Street, Monument Avenue, Patterson Avenue and Grove Avenue. An overhead concrete bridge for Cary Street Road had been constructed several years earlier. The ACL part of the new double track James River Branch left the ACL's main line at F. A. Tower (Falling Creek), 2.25 miles south of the old Clopton interchange yard and extended 6.06 miles to Pier 5 about the middle of the new James River Bridge. From Pier 5 the RF&P owned the branch 3.27 miles to Acca, along with the Acca wye track 0.29 miles to the RF&P main line over which connection was made with the tracks of the Richmond Terminal Railway Company. That portion of the old single track James River Branch which extended 2.96 miles from Clopton to Meadow Junction (the point where it joined the new double track James River Branch) was retained by the ACL and was used for switching service to industries located on the ACL in South Richmond. The new double track James River Branch was opened for service concurrent with the opening of operations at Broad Street Station on January 6, 1919.

During the single track era of the James River Branch, all trains were operated over the branch by the RF&P and freight traffic was interchanged between the RF&P and the ACL at the ACL's Clopton Yard. Pursuant to the ACL and RF&P's agreement to rebuild and double track the branch, the operation of the new branch was taken over by the ACL. Freight traffic between the ACL and RF&P was thereafter to be interchanged at the RF&P's Acca Yard and passenger traffic between the two railroads was interchanged at Richmond Terminal. All switching of ACL trains and cars at Acca was performed by RF&P crews. Acca Yard was enlarged to accommodate the new ACL traffic and on January 1, 1924 the RF&P opened a large new modern locomotive terminal immediately west of Acca Yard. This facility serviced and maintained all steam locomotives of the RF&P and handled the servicing and running repairs on the road steam locomotives of the ACL.

Following the relocation of the ACL's through freight trains and traffic to the RF&P's Acca facilities, the existing ACL yards were used to provide switching service and storage for the numerous industry warehouses served by the ACL in South Richmond. Clopton Yard was located 2.25 miles north of F. A. Tower and 3.29 Miles south of Byrd Street Station on the ACL's main line. The yard was located on the west side of the main line and there were a number of industries in the vicinity of Clopton served by the ACL crews working out of the South Richmond yards. A wye track was located just north of Clopton where the former

With its short train enveloped in its own smoke, an ACL 1500-series 4-6-2 hustles a freight extra, the "LCL hot shot", north of Collier Yard in February of 1943. (Robert S. Crockett Photo/William E. Griffin, Jr. Collection)

ACL northbound freight train No. 210, led by F7 No. 376 and three other F units, crosses Halifax Road crossing and is about to pass over the tracks of the N&W's belt line as its departs ACL's Collier Yard in Petersburg in July of 1966. Petersburg's Collier Yard was not a large facility on the ACL system but was a point of interchange with the N&W. The yard was substantially enlarged after the ACL and SAL created the SCL in 1967. (William E. Griffin, Jr. Photo)

single track line of the old James River Branch departed the ACL's main line for a distance of 2.96 miles to Meadow, where connection was made with the new double track James River Branch.

Approximately three miles north of Clopton on the ACL main line was Shops Yard, located at the intersection of Cowardin and Semmes Avenues and just south of the ACL's James River bridge. While the maintenance and servicing of road steam locomotives was moved to the RF&P's new Acca Locomotive Terminal in 1924, an engine house was retained at Shops to service the ACL's yard locomotives that worked South Richmond. Located at Shops were an office building and storeroom, three stall engine house (two used for locomotives), turntable and machine shop. The yard consisted of ten tracks, a rip track and engine service tracks. However, the primary function of Shops Yard was the interchange of ACL traffic with that of the C&O and Southern railways.

With the construction of the double track James River Branch, Broad Street Station and enlarged Acca facilities, there was little change in the ACL operations in Richmond until the 1960's. However, the transition from steam to diesel motive power had mandated the requirement for new mechanical facilities throughout the rail industry. In 1960 a committee of RF&P mechanical and engineering officials drew up a plan to consolidate all of the shops into a single, modern facility. Construction began immediately and on July 1, 1962, the new consolidated shop – known as Bryan Park Terminal – was opened for service. The four acre shop structure, located on the west side of Acca Yard, housed under one roof a new facility for heavy and running repairs to cars and the locomotives. All RF&P locomotives and road-freight and road-passenger ACL locomotives were given trip servicing, inspection and repair at the new shop. At that time, the ACL was operating about ten freight and ten passenger trains into Richmond on a daily basis.

As was the case at Richmond, the ACL's main line at Petersburg was built directly through the downtown area of the city and involved a substantial amount of street running. In 1895 a freight bypass was also built around the city of Petersburg. The cutoff left the old main line at Dunlop (north of Petersburg) extended west of the city and rejoined the main line at a new interlocking known as "BX" (north of today's Collier Yard). Through freights and "hot" through passenger trains bypassed the city. Other passenger trains stopped at the old ACL passenger station on Washington Street and also stopped at the N&W's station on River Street. Finally all passenger service was relocated to North Petersburg (Ettrick) when a new brick passenger station was built at that location. The final ACL station in Petersburg (the one used by Amtrak today) was built at Ettrick in 1955 adjacent to the 1942 station. Prior to the merger that created the Seaboard Coast Line Railroad there was no physical connection between the ACL and SAL at Petersburg. However, there was substantial interchange of freight traffic between the N&W and ACL at Collier Yard and Pocahontas Yard. Today, much of the former ACL has disappeared from Petersburg but Collier Yard remains as an interchange point with the Norfolk Southern and CSXT, the ACL belt line remains as CSXT's main line and the North Petersburg Station continues as the city's Amtrak station.

During the steam era and the early period of diesel operation, the ACL's peak season for freight traffic was during the winter months when perishables (vegetables and citrus fruits) were rushed from Florida to the northern markets. This traffic was either received from the Florida East Coast Railway at Jacksonville, Florida or originated on ACL lines in eastern and central Florida. It was forwarded in through trains over the ACL's double track main line from Florida to the RF&P at Richmond, thence to the Potomac Yard gateway where it was interchanged for shipment to various markets. For many years the ACL's scheduled fast or through freights originated southbound at Potomac Yard or Pinners Point and northbound at Montgomery, Alabama and Jacksonville, Florida. Much of the ACL northbound traffic routed over the Selma line to Pinners Point was then loaded onto steamship lines for shipment to both domestic and foreign ports.

Because of its easy grades on its main line between Richmond and Jacksonville, the ACL was unique among American railroads in its use for many years of the Pacific (4-6-2) type of steam locomotive as its standard motive power for both passenger and freight service. However, as the lengths of both freight and passenger trains increased, as well as the weights of their rolling stock and lading, the ACL found it necessary to resort to the expensive operating practice of double heading its Pacific steam locomotives to maintain schedules. To avoid the double heading of Pacifics, the ACL purchased twelve R-1 class 4-8-4's and assigned them to both freight and passenger service on its Richmond-Jacksonville main line.

When it came to passenger service, the ACL had early on established itself as the premier passenger service between Florida and the Northeast. From the earliest days of its existence, the ACL's seasonal *Florida Special* set the standard for luxurious travel by train. In addition to the *Special*, the ACL operated a number of popular trains such as the *Champion*, *Miamian*, *Havana Special*, *Vacationer*, *Palmetto* and *Everglades*. All

The ACL's belt line around Petersburg ultimately became a part of the railroad's main line. Between Dunlop and "BX" the line bridged the N&W's line to its Petersburg passenger station, the main line of the Seaboard Air Line Railway and the Appomattox River. ACL E6-A No. 523 is rolling a short passenger train across the belt line's Appomattox River bridge on June 23, 1947. (Bob's Photo Collection)

While the ACL's chief competitor, the Seaboard Air Line Railway, was experimenting with new diesel powered locomotives to meet it motive power requirements on its Florida trains, the ACL turned to the mechanical engineers at Baldwin Locomotive Works to develop a more powerful and efficient steam locomotive. Baldwin's answer would be twelve R-1 class 4-8-4s – the most powerful modern steam locomotives ever owned by the ACL. Numbered 1800–1811, these locomotives were delivered in 1938 and worked in both passenger and freight service between Richmond and Jacksonville. Here R-1 No. 1806 is rolling a southbound freight through Meadow in South Richmond on March 28, 1948. The original single-track James River Branch extended from the south end of the RF&P's Acca Yard to the ACL's Clopton Yard in South Richmond. When the James River Branch was double-tracked in 1916-1917, the line was extended south to FA Tower at Falling Creek on the ACL. A portion of the old single-track was left in place from Meadow to Clopton Yard and served as a connection to Clopton for ACL industrial crews working in South Richmond. (J. I. Kelly Photo/William E. Griffn, Jr. Collection)

of these trains operated though the Commonwealth of Virginia over the ACL and RF&P. The ACL's passenger route between Rocky Mount, North Carolina and Norfolk was essentially operated as a branch line service. ACL tracks only operated to Pinners Point where passengers detrained and were then transported across the Elizabeth River to Norfolk by ferry boat, and in the final years by motor bus. For many years the route was served by two sets of trains, one that operated at night (43-44) and another that operated during daylight hours (48-49). Passenger service came to an end on the Rocky Mount to Norfolk route in 1954. Passenger service survived as a first-class operation of the New York-Florida trains until the creation of Amtrak in 1971.

To begin the replacement of steam locomotives in passenger service, the ACL purchased two E3-A diesels from the Electro-Motive Corporation in 1939. Twenty-two slant nosed E6-A diesels and five E6-B booster units were ordered from EMD between 1940 and 1942 as the ACL rapidly converted its passenger motive power fleet to diesel locomotives. The E6-A's were numbered in the series 502-523 and the booster units were numbered 750-B to 754-B. They were initially assigned to the ACL's premier trains and worked exclusively in passenger service. Still working in the service for which it was designed we see E6-A No. 508 with an ACL passenger train at Broad Street Station in Richmond in July of 1958. (Bill McCoy Photo)

The ACL's other line into the Commonwealth of Virginia extended from Rocky Mount, North Carolina to Pinners Point at Portsmouth. For many years the ACL operated two sets of passenger trains over this line. One set operated at night (Trains 43-44) and the other operated during daylight hours (Trains 48-49). Under theatrics of smoke and exhaust on a frigid winter day, class P-5-B 4-6-2 No. 1668 gets underway with Train No. 49 on its late morning departure from Portsmouth. (L. D. Moore/William E. Griffin, Jr. Collection)

Looking west along Petersburg's Washington Street in 1951 we see the ACL's elegant 1903 passenger station. In the foreground is the Union Street grade crossing and to the left a corner of the freight station. In the distance beyond the station the main line tracked curved to the left in the direction of the Brown and Williamson Tobacco Factory. Classic 1950's era automobiles fill Washington Street in front of the station. (William E. Griffin, Jr. Collection)

The front of the ACL's freight station at Petersburg is seen in this photo taken from the corner of Washington and Sycamore streets. Looking west of Washington Street we see the passenger station just beyond the freight station. The freight station took up the entire city block from Sycamore Street to Union Street and the double track passed in front of the freight station. Note the cobble stone Washington Street east of the intersection and the exceptional array of classic automobiles in the scene. Both the freight and passenger stations on Washington Street were removed in 1955 to make way for new J. C. Penny and W. T. Grant department stores. (William E. Griffin, Jr. Collection)

The ACL's Shops Yard in Richmond was located on the old main line at the intersection of Cowardin and Semmes Avenues and just south of the ACL's bridge over the James River. While the maintenance and servicing of ACL's road locomotives was moved to the RF&P's Acca Locomotive Terminal in 1924, an engine house was retained at Shops to service the ACL's yard locomotives that worked South Richmond. Also located at Shops were an office building, storeroom, three-stall engine house, turntable and machine shop. The yard consisted of 10 tracks, a rip track and engine service tracks. However, the main function of Shops Yard was the interchange of ACL traffic with that of the C&O and Southern railroads. The ACL interchanged with the C&O at the C&O's Second Street Yard located on the north side of the river. The Southern Railway's Richmond to Danville line passed under the ACL just east of Shops. The Southern's Belle Isle Yard was located at a lower level from Shops and an interchange track between the two railroads ran from the north end of Shops down a steep hill to the west end of the Belle Isle Yard. In this view looking north towards the Richmond skyline, we see all of the facilities located at the ACL's Shops Yard. (William E. Griffin, Jr. Collection)

Like its longtime competitor the Atlantic Coast Line Railroad, the Seaboard Air Line Railway operated two main line routes into the Commonwealth of Virginia. Also like the ACL, one route led to Tidewater and the other to Richmond. The SAL's line to the Tidewater area was built by one of the nation's earliest railroads and its construction began a rivalry with the ACL that would last for over 100 years. The SAL's line to Richmond was the last railroad to be built into that city and the resolution of a dispute involving its construction would set the pattern for SAL and ACL operations until their merger in 1967.

The SAL's earliest predecessor company, the Portsmouth and Roanoke Railroad, was incorporated in Virginia on March 8, 1832 and in North Carolina on January 9, 1833 to build a railroad from Portsmouth to Weldon, North Carolina on the Roanoke River. Construction of the line began in 1833; the first tracks being laid with longitudinal wooden stringers covered with strips of strap iron. By July of 1834, the line had been extended from Portsmouth through the western edge of the Great Dismal Swamp to Suffolk. In the absence of locomotives, operations were commenced with horse-drawn coaches making two daily trips. The first locomotive arrived on September 4, 1834 aboard a packet schooner from England. Named the *John Barnett*, this five-ton locomotive was soon handling trains between Portsmouth and Suffolk in an hour and fifteen minutes at the previously unheard of speed of 15 mph. The line was completed to the Roanoke River in 1836 and the river was bridged to reach Weldon in 1837. However, the railroad was poorly constructed and soon failed. In 1843 it was sold in a foreclosure sale on behalf of its creditors who promptly began removing the railroad's track. By 1846, operations south of Boykins were discontinued and the railroad was sold in another foreclosure sale to the Commonwealth of Virginia's Board of Public Works.

Map by Stanley W. Short, William E. Griffin, Jr. Collection

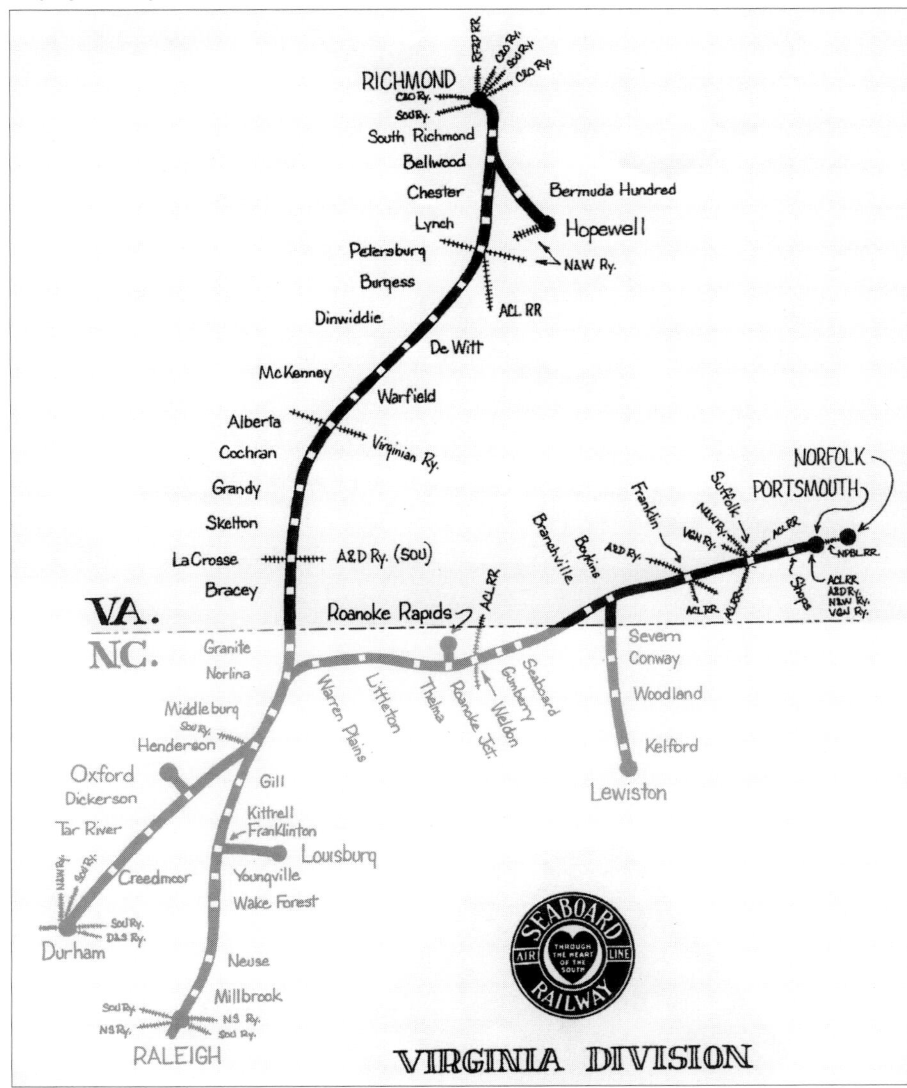

A new railroad – the Seaboard and Roanoke Railroad – was incorporated in 1846 to rebuild the line from Portsmouth to the Virginia-Carolina state line. Another company – the Roanoke Railroad – rebuilt the railroad from the state line, near Margaretville (now Margaret), to Weldon. This railroad was acquired by the Seaboard and Roanoke in 1849 and by 1851 the entire line from Portsmouth to Weldon was rebuilt, this time with the hazardous strap rail replaced by "T" iron rail imported from England. Two years later, the line of the Seaboard and Roanoke Railroad made connection with the Raleigh and Gaston Railroad. The connection of these two railroads established an unbroken rail line from Raleigh, North Carolina to the ports of Portsmouth and Norfolk for conveyance of North Carolina products. Further expansion was deferred during the years of the War Between the States. Expansion resumed after the war and in 1877 the line of the Raleigh and Gaston was extended south to Hamlet, North Carolina.

In 1893, five railroads whose lines extended from Portsmouth through the Carolinas and Georgia to Atlanta formed an unincorporated association known as the Seaboard Air Line System. The words "Air Line" came into the Seaboard's name through one of its predecessor companies, the Raleigh and Augusta Air-Line Railroad. It was the first recorded application of the words to a railroad. During that period, the words "air line" were used to signify the shortest distance between two points and may have derived from the expression "as the crow flies". In any event, the use of the name by the railroad at this time predated the Wright brothers' first flight at Kitty Hawk, North Carolina by 32 years.

The SAL extended its line of railroad to Richmond in the spring of 1900. The new railroad was greeted with celebration - and controversy. Since 1877 the owners of the SAL's predecessor roads had agreed not to operate rail or steamship service to either Richmond or West Point, Virginia in exchange for an agreement by the Southern Railway's predecessor companies not to offer service into Norfolk or Portsmouth. When this agreement was breached by the SRR in 1896, the SAL retaliated by inaugurating a new steamship service between Baltimore and Richmond and set out to extend its rail line from Ridgeway Junction (now Norlina, North Carolina) to Richmond.

Extension of the line to Richmond was accomplished by the acquisition of the Richmond, Petersburg & Carolina Railroad. The RP&C was the successor to the franchise of the Virginia and Carolina Railroad, a company that had been chartered in 1882 to build a railroad from Richmond to a connection with the Raleigh and Gaston. When the V&CRR failed in 1892 without laying a single mile of track the franchise was purchased by the city of Petersburg in a foreclosure sale. In 1897, DeWitt Smith, who had purchased the franchise from the city approached Richmond banker John Skelton Williams for financial backing to build the line.

By 1898, the Williams banking group, working in concert with banking associates from Baltimore, had acquired a controlling interest in the Seaboard Air-Line System of railroads. They had also acquired the franchise for the RP&C and completed construction in 1899 of line from Petersburg to DeWitt. In 1900 the RP&C was completed and was operating from Richmond to a connection with the Raleigh and Gaston in North Carolina. Upon completion of the RP&C, by previous agreement, the Sea-

Looking north from the North Boulevard bridge onto the SAL's Hermitage Yard in the early 1950's. To the left are the main line tracks of the SAL to Main Street Station and the RF&P's lead tracks to Broad Street Station. To the right is the new brick yard office building, water tank and coaling tower for steam locomotives. In the distance is the new diesel shop. (Edward D. Patterson Photo, William E. Griffin, Jr. Collection)

board Air Line Railway Company became the lessee of the road, and on April 10, 1900, by an act of the Virginia General Assembly, the RP&C changed its name to the Seaboard Air Line Railway and became part of a chain of railroads that stretched from Richmond to Tampa, Florida.

However, Williams realized that direct rail service through the Washington gateway to the Northeast would be essential if his new rail system was to successfully compete with the existing rail systems of the ACL and Southern Railway. This would require that the SAL obtain satisfactory arrangements for its through traffic to be handled by the RF&P north of Richmond. As outlined in the RF&P chapter in this book, when the SAL was denied arrangements it deemed desirable by the ACL-controlled RF&P, Williams used his considerable political influence to have the RF&P and ACL drop their opposition and allow the SAL to use the RF&P for its traffic to Washington and beyond. The SAL's connection with the RF&P at Hermitage, four miles north of the James River, was opened and interchange between the railroads began on July 1, 1900.

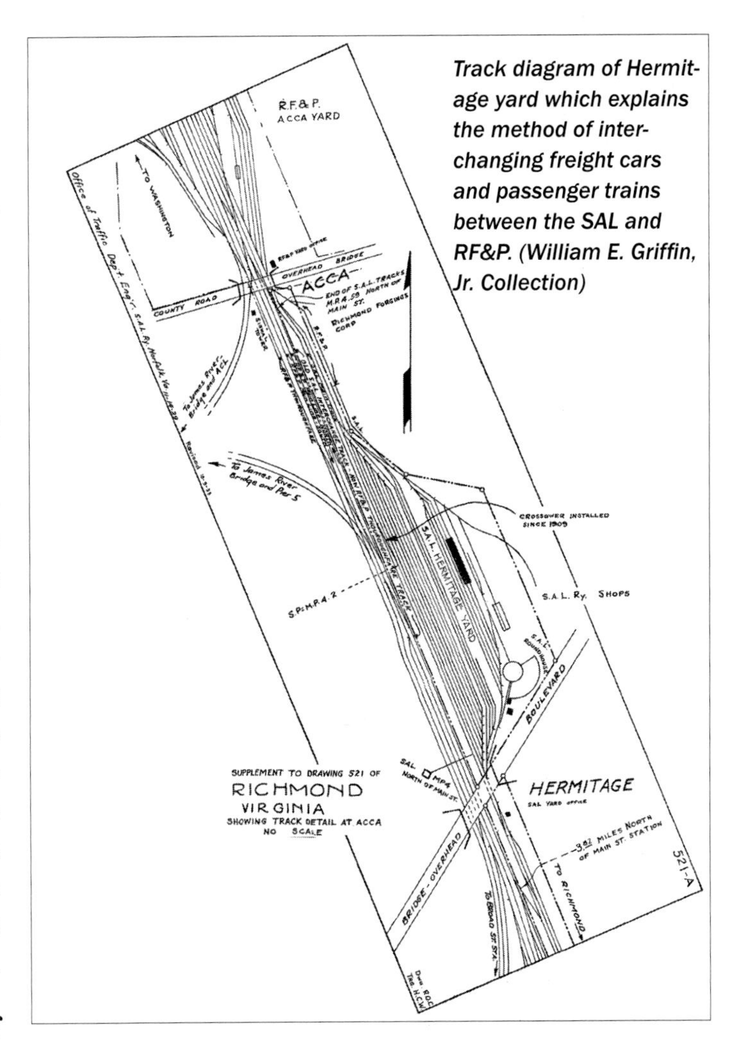

Track diagram of Hermitage yard which explains the method of interchanging freight cars and passenger trains between the SAL and RF&P. (William E. Griffin, Jr. Collection)

All SAL operations in the Commonwealth of Virginia were supervised by the Virginia Operating Division that was headquartered in Raleigh, North Carolina and was responsible for the operation of "all lines north of Raleigh". The home terminal of all road engines and train crews was located at Raleigh. The Virginia Division was divided into the Richmond Subdivision that supervised operations on the lines between Hermitage and Norlina, North Carolina; the Portsmouth Subdivision that supervised operations between Portsmouth and Norlina; and the Norlina Subivision that supervised operations between Norlina and Raleigh.

As other steam locomotive wait their turn for service, SAL F-7 class 0-6-0 No. 1108 is being loaded with coal at the Hermitage Yard coaling tower. Built in 1900, the tower had the capacity of 1,000 tons of coal. The SAL's F-7 class of switchers were nationally recognized as one of the most efficient and economical 0-6-0 type switchers ever designed by American locomotive builders. Built by Baldwin, Nos. 1101-1125 were delivered in 1927 with Nos. 1126-1150 delivered the following year. (D. Wallace Johnson Photo, William E. Griffin, Jr. Collection)

The tracks of the Richmond Subdivision entered the Commonwealth at the Roanoke River, about two miles south of Bracey and extended for approximately 88 miles to Hermitage.

In a view looking north at Hermitage Yard we see the roundhouse, water tank, yard office and the North Boulevard bridge. The Hermitage roundhouse had 16 stalls and an electrically operated 100-foot turntable. Hermitage was the northern terminus of the railroad and the north end of the yard joined the south end of the RF&P's Acca Yard. A relatively small yard that could not be enlarged, it was closed in 1970 following the SAL and ACL merger when the new SCL moved the functions formerly performed at Hermitage to the RF&P's Acca Yard. (Edward D. Patterson Photo, William E. Griffin, Jr. Collection)

At LaCrosse (Mile Post 79), the SAL crossed the single track main line of the Atlantic and Danville Railway. At Mile Post 61, the SAL passed under the main line of the Virginian Railway at Alberta. At Mile Post 31, the SAL bridged the freight belt line of the N&W at Burgess. The SAL passed under the ACL and over the N&W passenger line at Petersburg, then between Petersburg and Richmond, the ACL passed over the SAL at Lynch and the SAL passed over the ACL at Chester. The SAL interchanged with the A&D at LaCrosse; the VGN at Alberta; the Southern at Rocketts Junction (Richmond) and the C&O at Brown Street (Richmond). The important Hopewell Subdivision of the SAL's Virginia Division extended from Bellwood (located at approximately eight miles south of Richmond) for a distance of 16 miles to the city of Hopewell. The SAL chartered the Prince George & Chesterfield Railway in 1929 to build the railroad from a connection with the main line at Bellwood to handle traffic from the important industrial complex at Hopewell.

Hermitage Yard was the principal SAL yard in Richmond and was the northern terminus of the railroad. The north end of Hermitage Yard connected end to end with the south end of the RF&P's Acca Yard. Hermitage yard had 20 yard tracks; a coach shed 300 feet long and 32 feet wide; a 16-stall brick roundhouse; a 100-foot electrically operated turntable; and, 1,000-ton capacity coal chute. Following the dieselization of motive power, a diesel service building, wash rack and fueling facilities were built immedi-

SAL FT diesels are parked beside the retired Hermitage Yard coaling tower and water tank. The SAL acquired its first road freight diesel locomotives in June 1942 with the delivery of six semi-permanently coupled A-B sets of EMD FT's. Six additional sets of A-B-B-A FT's were delivered in 1943 followed by ten A-B sets in 1944. All were delivered in a modified version of the "citrus" paint scheme applied to the passenger units. Between 1948 and 1949, they were repainted in what became the standard SAL freight paint scheme of Pullman Green car bodies with a wide yellow stripe bordered by orange pinstripes. (Edward D. Patterson Photo, William E. Griffin, Jr. Collection)

Southbound Red Ball freight No. 89 is pulling out of Hermitage Yard in July 1947 on a run that will take it to Norlina, Raleigh, Hamlet, Monroe and Charlotte, North Carolina. Motive power for the train is provided by R-1 class 2-6-6-4 No. 2502. The SAL owned five (Nos. 2500-2504) of these single expansion articulated type locomotives that were built by Baldwin in 1935 and they were immediately put into fast freight service between Richmond and Hamlet. The locomotives were so successful that the SAL purchased five more 2-6-6-4's from Baldwin in 1937. These locomotives were designated as the R-2 class and were numbered 2505-2509. The locomotives could easily handle 2700-ton trains between Richmond and Hamlet and were even used on heavy passenger trains during the winter months. When the SAL dieselized its operations it sold all of these locomotives to the B&O RR in 1947. (August A. Thieme, Jr. Photo, William E. Griffin, Jr. Collection)

ately north of the yard office. A new two-story red brick yard office was built at Hermitage in 1959. Continuous yard service was maintained at the yard. However, Hermitage was a relatively small yard with limited track capacity and, due to its geographic location, could not be enlarged. It could not be extended south due to the Boulevard Bridge or to the north because of RF&P's Acca Yard. Hermitage Yard would be closed and its operations moved to the RF&P's Acca Yard following the merger of the ACL and SAL that created the Seaboard Coast Line Railroad.

The SAL's Brown Street Yard was located at Mile Post 0.06 North, just north of the Main Street Passenger Station, with yard tracks on both the west and east side of the main line. Primarily used as an industrial marshalling yard, it had a total of 16 yard tracks. The west side, known as the "old yard" had a track capacity for 556 cars. The east side of the yard had three tracks with the capacity for 80 cars. The Brown Street yard office was a one-story brick building with a locker room and washroom on the north end of the building for enginemen and trainmen that worked assignments at the yard. All SAL road trains in and out of Richmond passed through Brown Street Yard and there were daily pickups and set-offs by the road switchers and through freight trains. Brown Street Yard was located adjacent to the C&O's 17th Street Yard. From the east yard at Brown Street, switching leads connected with the C&O interchange tracks that consisted of two delivery and two receiving tracks that had a capacity of 45 cars each. All SAL interchange with the C&O took place in the 17th Street Yard. The SAL yard crews at Brown Street also classified the interchange traffic received from the C&O for pickup by the outbound road crews leaving Hermitage.

The final SAL yard at Richmond was known as South Yard and it was located approximately halfway between Main Street Station and south yard limit board of Richmond Terminal. It was the smallest of the SAL's Richmond yards with just six classification tracks and capacity of a little over 200 cars. There was also a maze of storage and industrial tracks serving more than 20 separate industries in South Richmond. The yard crews at South Yard assembled cars picked up from the various industries at South Yard and then moved them to Brown Street. All yard crews working at South Yard went on and off duty at Brown Street. In addition to the industrial switching, crews at South Yard also handled the interchange of freight traffic with the Southern Railway at a point near the south end of the James River Bridge between Stewart Street and Rocketts Junction.

Initially, SAL passenger operations in Richmond were handled at Main Street Station. Jointly owned and operated by the SAL and C&O, the first SAL passenger train arrived at the new station on November 27, 1901. Interestingly, while Main Street Station served as the SAL passenger station for the traveling public, the actual interchange of all passenger trains between the SAL and the RF&P occurred at Hermitage, 3.4 miles north of the station. Since the tracks between Hermitage and Main Street Station were SAL tracks, the trains were considered to be SAL trains and were operated by the SAL between those points. However, it was the practice that the train crews for both roads changed at Main Street Station and RF&P train crews handled the trains between Hermitage and Main Street governed by SAL operating rules. SAL and RF&P engine crews and their locomotives did change at Hermitage and the engine crews handled their locomotives to and from their respective terminals and the interchange point. This division of functions and delay in operations ended in 1959 when the SAL discontinued its use of Main Street Station and moved its passenger operations to Broad Street Station. The SAL became a one-third owner in Richmond Terminal Company that operated Broad Street Station and commenced operations into the station on April 26, 1959. At that time, the SAL was operating 14 passenger trains into the city of Richmond. Because of the unique loop track arrangement at Broad Street Station, all trains of the ACL and RF&P were operated through the station in the same direction. This would not be the case with the SAL trains. The SAL had to operate its trains through the station via the south end which necessitated a back-in and back-out movement. The usual rear-end and head-end switching performed at Broad Street Station was reversed for SAL trains since northbound trains had to back-in and southbound trains had to back-out.

All of the premier SAL passenger trains passed over the tracks of the Virginia Division. They included the New York to Florida trains such as the seasonal all-Pullman *Orange Blossom Special*, *Southern States Special*, The *Palmland*, The *Sunland*, and the streamliners *The Silver Meteor* and *The Silver Star*. The was also the Atlanta and Birmingham trains such as *The Robert E Lee*, the *Cotton States Special* and the streamliner *The Silver Comet*. Local passenger trains as well as the Passenger, Mail and Express Train Nos. 3 and 4 made daily runs over the Division. These trains were able to maintain their schedules over the single track Richmond Subdivision of the Virginia Division thanks to the SAL's decision to install the first electronic centralized traffic system in the Southeastern United States on the Richmond Subdivision in the 1940's. Directed from the train dispatcher's office in Raleigh, the CTC system was superimposed on the SAL's existing automatic signal system.

SAL Q-3 class 2-8-2 No. 370 is set to depart Brown Street Yard after stopping to make a pickup to fill out its train. To the right in the photo is the SAL Brown Street yard office and the C&O's 17th Street Yard. The SAL Brown Street Yard was located adjacent to the C&O's 17th Street Yard and switching leads on the east side of the yard connected to the C&O interchange tracks. All interchange between the SAL and C&O occurred in the 17th Street Yard. Of 170 Mikado, or 2-8-2 type steam locomotives, 117 were of the Q-3 class design as delivered by both the American and Baldwin Locomotive Works between 1923 and 1926. Essentially a modified version of the USRA light Mikado, they were equipped with Vanderbilt tenders, stokers and a trailing truck booster that increased their tractive effort to 65,200 pounds. The feature that distinguished them from all other locomotives operating in the Southeast was the placement of their cross-compound air pumps on the front of the smokebox over the headlight that had been lowered below center. (Anthony Dementi Photo, William E. Griffn, Jr. Collection)

There were two other distinctive features of the SAL's presence in the city of Richmond. Just south of Main Street Station, the SAL tracks passed through the middle level of Richmond's unique triple crossing at 16th and Dock Streets, with the C&O viaduct of James River Division above and the tracks of the Southern Railway's Richmond Division at ground level. It is believed to be the only point in the nation where the trains of three separate railroads could cross each other at the same time and over separate tracks. The other distinctive feature was the SAL's last general office building that was located on West Broad Street. The SAL moved its general office from Portsmouth to Richmond in 1958 and, when it was opened on August 22, 1958, it was the largest office building in the city of Richmond.

The tracks of the Portsmouth Subdivision entered the Commonwealth of Virginia between Margaret, North Carolina and Branchville, Virginia and extended for approximately 60 miles to Portsmouth, passing through Boykins, Franklin and Suffolk. At Boykins, a branch line designated as the Lewiston Subdivision, extended from a connection with the SAL main line at Boykins for 89 miles to Lewiston, North Carolina.

The SAL could interchange with the A&D at Franklin; with all lines entering Suffolk (ACL, N&W, VGN, A&D) and had direct or indirect connection with all carrier lines entering the port of Portsmouth (ACL, N&W, VGN, A&D, and N&PBL).

Unlike the Richmond Subdivision that was equipped with CTC during the 1940's, movements over the long 115-mile Portsmouth Subdivision, called "the long barrel" and "the dark country" by SAL railroaders, were authorized by timetable and train orders issued by train dispatcher at Raleigh. However, the SAL did operate fast "Red Ball" freight over the single track Portsmouth Subdivision. During the 1930's, the service was performed by Train Nos. 85 (the *Merchandiser*) and 82 (the *Courier*) that operated between Shops (Portsmouth) and Birmingham via Atlanta. Local freights Nos. 60-61 were operated daily except Sunday between Norlina and Portsmouth. By the 1960's, a single daily through freight (which retained the numbers 85 and 82) operated over the subdivision in each direction.

Passenger service over the Portsmouth Subdivision consisted of the *Cotton States Special* (Train Nos. 17 and 18) and Passenger, Mail and Express Trains 13 and 14. Portsmouth Subdi-

Built to jointly serve the SAL and C&O railroads, the Main Street Station was designed by the Wilson Brothers of Philadelphia and was a classic example of the French Renaissance railway structure in the Southern United States. With its orange-brown Pompeian brick, Spanish tile roof, ornate clock tower and decorated gables, the station opened on Thanksgiving Day 1901 to rave reviews. In this view, SAL train No. 107 – The Sun Queen – is leaving Main Street on its southbound trip in 1944 behind M-2 class 4-8-2 No. 263. Formerly known as the Southern States Special, Train No. 107 operated daily between New York and Miami. (August A. Thieme, Jr. Photo, William E. Griffn, Jr. Collection)

SAL E-7 No. 3027 is shown during its station stop at Main Street Station with its southbound passenger train. The SAL platform was located on the west side of the station and the C&O platform was on the east side of the building. (Wiley M. Bryan Photo, William E. Griffn, Jr. Collection)

vision passenger trains with through coaches and sleepers were scheduled to connect at Norlina with mainline trains operating between Richmond and points south. In later years, the southern terminus of the Portsmouth trains was changed from Norlina to Raleigh. By the 1960's, Trains Nos. 17 and 18 (renamed the *Tidewater*) were the only passenger trains operating on the Portsmouth Subdivision.

For many years, the SAL's headquarters building and principal shops were located at Portsmouth. Located at High and Water Streets, the SAL's former headquarters building in Portsmouth was built in 1894 and expanded in 1915. It also served as a passenger station and its proximity to the Elizabeth River permitted passengers on SAL trains to make connections for Norfolk and beyond via Portsmouth and Norfolk ferries which berthed just beyond the building. Ticket offices, waiting and baggage rooms occupied the first floor of the building while SAL corporate and operations offices were on the upper floors. In its heyday more than 600 SAL employees worked in the building. The last major group was the accounting department, which was transferred to Richmond in 1958.

The SAL station at High and Water Streets was the "end of the line" for Portsmouth Subdivision passenger trains. Upon arrival the locomotive and cars were pulled over to the shops by yard crews to be serviced for the outbound trip. The outbound passenger trains were placed at the passenger station by yard crews. Crawford Street crossed the station tracks just west of the platform and when the head ends of the trains were too long to clear the crossing, the train was cut and the head end was placed in a the station track adjacent to the one on which the rear of the train was standing. When the train was loaded preparatory to departure the outbound road crews pulled ahead over the switch to the track on which the rear of the train was standing and then backed to a coupling with the train, made it solid and departed.

Portsmouth was formerly the main locomotive repair shop for the northern lines but in 1936 it was converted to the main passenger car repair shop when the locomotive classified repair work was transferred to the Jacksonville, Florida shops. When built in 1915, the SAL Portsmouth erecting shop was one of the most modern backshops in the country. The large 332'x178' erecting shop was used for heavy repairs to steam locomotives and once held locomotive, erecting, machine and blacksmith shops. After 1936 one bay of the erecting shop with its 15 tracks was used as a coach shop with a machine shop located in the other two bays. There was a passenger car paint shop and the wheel shop supplied wheels for Portsmouth, Hamlet, Hermitage and other points on the north end. The locomotive roundhouse at Portsmouth originally had 23 stalls and a 68-foot hand opened turntable. Following the transfer of the classified locomotive repair work to Jacksonville, only running repair work was performed at Portsmouth. By 1944, the roundhouse had been reduced to 8 stalls.

In the years following the SAL and ACL merger that created the SCL Railroad, a large portion of the SAL's trackage in the Commonwealth of Virginia was abandoned. However, the corridor from Collier Yard in Petersburg to just south of the Virginia-North Carolina border (which is still owned by CSX) has been proposed for use as a part of the Southeast High Speed Rail line. Hence, the possibility exists that the old SAL Richmond Subdivision may once again be used as a rail line.

The Bellwood operator steps out of his office to inspect the passage of northbound Passenger, Mail and Express train No. 4 that has just passed under the U.S. Route 1 overpass. E-4 No. 3004 leads the three E-unit consist all painted in the citrus paint scheme. The SAL acquired its first diesel electric road locomotives in 1938 to power the new Orange Blossom Special. These E-4 diesels were built by the Electro-Motive Corporation and had two 1000-horsepower "V" type, two cycle, 12-cylinder engines, two EMC-type 600-volt main generators, and four EMC 600-volt traction motors. Each unit had two 6-wheel trucks with 36-inch diameter wheels. The units were delivered in three A-B-A sets and the main parts of all units were interchangeable. (Anthony Dementi Photo, William E. Griffin, Jr. Collection)

Bellwood was an important point for freight operations on the Richmond Subdivision. Here the SAL's main line was joined by the important industrial branch line to the Hopewell industrial complex. Connection was also made with the U. S. Army Quartermaster Supply Depot. In this view, Extra 4007 North is departing Bellwood with FTA No. 4007 and one FTB unit en-route to Hermitage with a merchandise freight. (Anthony Dementi Photo, William E. Griffin, Jr. Collection)

Trains entered the city of Petersburg from the north via a high bridge that spanned both the Appomattox River and the tracks of the N&W's line to its passenger station. In this photo, Q-3 class 2-8-2 No. 447 storms across the Petersburg high bridge with Extra 447 North on February 3, 1946. (August A. Thieme, Jr. Photo, William E. Griffin, Jr. Collection)

In an extremely rare photo, this is the SAL station at Dunlop Street. Locomotive Fireman Wiley M. Bryan remembered that when a long northbound passenger train stopped at the station, the locomotive would occasionally be stopped on the high bridge. On June 1, 1944, the SAL closed its station at Dunlop and opened a new station further south that fronted on Commerce Street. (John W. Barriger Collection, St Louis Mercantile Library)

The new colonial style SAL station on Commerce Street was located some 1,700-feet south of the former station at Dunlop. The new station allowed trains to stop on a straight section of track (Dunlop was on a curve). It also facilitated the movement of trains because they could now stop clear of the north end of the passing track, thus permitting the passing of trains stopped in the station. (William E. Griffn, Jr. Photo)

In a classic Wiley Bryan photo, we see Q-3 class 2-8-2 No. 355 taking on water at McKenney for it northbound train. The water column shown in this photo was used by northbound trains. Southbound trains took on water from the water tank visible just down the tracks. McKenney was an important location for crews to fill their locomotive's tenders with water. By the 1940's, the doubleheading of Q-3's was a frequent operating practice as the freight equipment became heavier and the trains were longer. The doubleheading of Mikado locomotives was eliminated first by the R-1 class 2-6-6-4's and finally by the replacement of steam with diesel electric locomotives. (Wiley M. Bryan, William E. Griffin, Jr. Collection)

SAL train No. 108, the northbound Southern States Special, races past the station at McKenney with three E-4's running in the typical SAL "elephant style". The town of McKenney was named for William R. McKenney, an attorney who represented the RP&C RR at its inception in 1898. The towns of DeWitt and Skelton could also trace their names to SAL officials. (Wiley M. Bryan Photo, William E. Griffin, Jr. Collection)

Alberta was an important location on the SAL as it served as an interchange point with the Virginian Railway. The station was manned by SAL employees and was located on ground level adjacent to the SAL main line. The VGN passed over the SAL on elevated tracks and stairs behind the station led to the VGN's platform above. Express and baggage were raised or lowered by a hand cranked elevator that was housed in the wooden tower shown in this photo. (Edward D. Patterson Photo, William E. Griffin, Jr. Collection)

While road switchers and some through freights stopped at Alberta, it could also be a roaring fast place as hot shot freights and passenger trains sped through town. FTA No. 4001 won't be stopping in Alberta as it speeds its southbound freight past the station in May of 1951. (Robert G. Lewis Photo, William E. Griffin, Jr. Collection)

Located in Southampton County on the Blackwater River at that county's line with Isle of Wight County, the town of Franklin was an important source of freight traffic on the SAL's Portsmouth Subdivision. The large Union Camp Corporation was located in Franklin and the A&D Railway and the SAL used joint trackage to serve the industry. The SAL's passenger station in Franklin was a handsome facility and for many years it had a tower that is visible behind the locomotive in this photo. The train is SAL No. 13, which operated between Portsmouth and Norlina and it is shown making a stop in Franklin on October 10, 1948 . The locomotive is P class 4-6-2 No. 861 which was one of the ten Pacific type engines purchased by the SAL in 1911. Originally in the number series 90-99, the SAL purchased twelve more of this type of locomotive in 1912-13. In 1929 they were renumbered in the series 851-870. They were the standard SAL passenger locomotives until replaced by the Mountain type steam locomotives. (H. Reid Photo, William E. Griffin, Jr. Collection)

Towers were commonly found the SAL stations on the Portsmouth Subdivision and they may have been added to the structures to give the operators a better view of the train operation that was governed by timetable and train order. Another tower was found on the Suffolk passenger station that was shared by the SAL and the VGN. Built in 1885 and remodeled in 1920, the Suffolk station was typical of the 19th century style. Located in downtown Suffolk, the station fell into a state of disrepair until restored by the Suffolk-Nansemond Historical Society and city of Suffolk with the help of grants and fundraising projects. In this view we again see SAL Train No. 13 arriving at the station on December 29, 1949. This time the motive power is provided by M-2 class 4-8-2 No. 269. The Mountain type 4-8-2 type steam locomotives first came to the SAL in 1914 with the delivery of ten locomotives from the Richmond Works of the American Locomotive Company. Designed for heavy passenger train service, locomotives of the M class (200-214), M-1 class (215-224) and M-2 class (235-270) worked throughout the SAL system. (H. Reid Photo, William E. Griffin, Jr. Collection)

Built in 1894 and enlarged in 1915, the SAL's passenger station and headquarters office building at Portsmouth was located at High and Water Streets. Ticket offices, waiting rooms and baggage rooms were located on the ground floor. SAL corporate and operations offices occupied the upper floors. The last group of SAL employees to occupy the offices was moved to Richmond in 1958 when the SAL built a new consolidated office on Broad Street in Richmond. This view of the Portsmouth station and office building was taken on September 12, 1947. (H. Reid Photo, William E. Griffin, Jr. Collection)

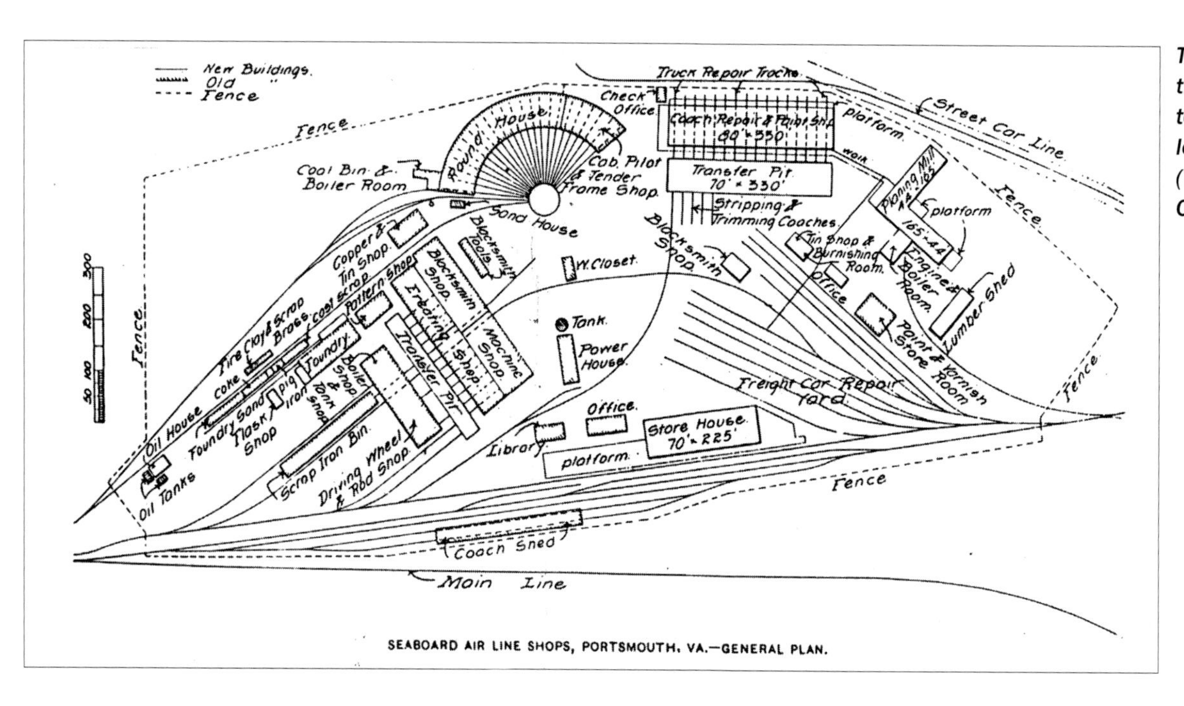

The general plan and track diagram of the extensive shops that were located at Portsmouth. (William E. Griffin, Jr. Collection)

The SAL posed the extremes of steam locomotive development in front of the Portsmouth shops in 1940. The replica of Raleigh and Gaston RR 4-2-0 locomotive The Tornado was built at the Raleigh shops in 1892 under the supervision of the railroad's Master Mechanic, who remembered the details of the original locomotive that was built in 1839. The replica of the 1839 locomotive is posed beside R-2 class 2-6-6-4, the last articulated locomotive purchased by the SAL. (William E. Griffin, Jr. Collection)

Taking water at the Portsmouth shops is F-7 class 0-6-0 No. 1118 on May 13, 1951. (H. Reid Photo, William E. Griffin, Jr. Collection)

Originally the Portsmouth roundhouse had stalls for 23 locomotives. The building was downsized to eight stalls following the transfer of classified repair work to Jacksonville in 1936. Four of stalls are occupied with steam locomotives on August 10, 1949. In the foreground is the 68-foot hand-operated turntable. (H. Reid Photo, William E. Griffin, Jr. Collection)

The SAL owned most of the waterfront land at Portsmouth along the west side of the Elizabeth River from South Street north to and including the southern part of Crawford Bay. On this land the SAL located its various warehouses and terminals with track facilities over Crawford Street. This is a view of SAL piers 8 and 9 at Portsmouth. (William E. Griffin, Jr. Collection)

Until its demise in October 1991, the Richmond, Fredericksburg and Potomac Railroad had the distinction of being the oldest American railroad still operating under its original name and charter. Formed when rail transportation was still in its earliest stage of development, the RF&P was the sixth railroad to be chartered in Virginia and only the third to operate its trains with steam power. When CSX Corporation acquired the railroad assets and operations of the RF&P in 1991 it brought to an end the RF&P's remarkable achievement of continuously operating its rail property with its own organization during the 157 years of its corporate existence. The RF&P was also notable as one of our country's most successful short line railroads. With only 113 miles of main line track, it was one of the shortest railroads in the nation. However, the RF&P's importance resulted from its strategic location, which formed the principal route through which the commerce of the northern and southern cities of the Atlantic Seaboard region could flow.

On February 25, 1834, the RF&P was granted a charter by Act of the General Assembly of Virginia. That charter provided for the construction of a railroad from some point in the city of Richmond to some point within the corporate limits of Fredericksburg, with the authority to extend the railroad "... should it be deemed advisable, to the Potomac River or some creek thereof". The charter also provided for immunity from competition in passenger traffic between Richmond and Washington for a period of thirty years. A year after the original charter was granted, the Commonwealth of Virginia determined to take a direct fiscal interest in the RF&P and the Board of Public Works authorized the commonwealth's subscription to two-fifths of the capital stock. Private subscriptions accounted for more than three-fifths and the commonwealth actually acquired 2,752 shares of the stock. The commonwealth retained ownership of RF&P stock and it proved to be a most valuable investment.

The line was opened to Fredericksburg, 61 miles, on January 23, 1837. A stage line from there to the mouth of the Potomac Creek connected the railroad with a line of steam boats to Washington via the Potomac River. Soon after the line had been opened to Fredericksburg, it was decided to extend it across the Rappahannock River to reach one of the steamboat landings on the Potomac River. Surveys convinced the RF&P that the best route and deeper water could be obtained by going to a landing at Aquia Creek, located fourteen miles from Fredericksburg. The line was opened to Aquia in November of 1842. The RF&P had now established its line as an important link in the through route of travel from the South to Baltimore, passengers being handled by rail on the RF&P from Richmond to Aquia Creek, thence by steamboats to Washington, thence by rail (the Baltimore and Ohio Railroad) to Baltimore. The railroad even acquired a controlling interest in the Potomac Steamboat Company that provided the steamboats used in the service.

Any plans to further extend the RF&P were abruptly halted by the start of the War Between the States, with portions of the railroad alternately in possession of Union and/or Confederate forces until March of 1865 when the line was completely destroyed between Fredericksburg and Richmond. However, by September of 1865 the bridges had been rebuilt and the main line was again reopened between Richmond and Aquia Creek. Following the war the rail systems along the Atlantic Seaboard were finally linked together.

Connection of the rail lines in Richmond was achieved by construction of the Richmond, Fredericksburg and Potomac and Richmond and Petersburg Railroad Connection Company. Chartered on March 3, 1866, the Connection Railroad, as it was called, opened for service in April of 1867 and was operated under lease by the RF&P. Only one and a fourth miles long, the Connection Railroad joined the Richmond and Petersburg RR by a trestle at 5th and Byrd Streets, necessitating a tunnel 900 feet long at Gamble's Hill, and its track extended as far as a trestle at Second and Belvidere streets. The track was laid along Byrd Street to Grace Street to a connection with the RF&P at Broad and Pine streets. For a distance of one fourth mile, the grade of the line was nearly 2.2 per cent, quite steep for railroad operations in a city. Cary, Main, Franklin and Grace – all important streets – were crossed at grade. The RF&P did not abandon its operations on Broad Street at this time (with its offices, shops and passenger station located at 8th and Broad streets in downtown Richmond) but all through trains were handled over the Connection Railroad until 1919.

The RF&P made connection with the northern lines at Quantico. At a special meeting the stockholders of the RF&P authorized construction under the Company's charter of a 10-mile extension from Brooke for the purpose of making connection near Quantico Creek with the Alexandria and Fredericksburg Railway and establishing a new and more desirable connection with the Potomac Steamboat Company. As the extension of 10 miles permitted under the Company's charter fell a mile or two short of reaching the new wharf at Quantico Creek and the point of connection with the A&F Railway, the RF&P arranged for the additional mileage by construction of the Potomac Railroad Company. The RF&P operated the Potomac Railroad Company and advanced funds for its construction. The line to Quantico Creek and the new connection with the steamboat company were opened for traffic on May 1, 1872 and the RF&P abandoned its former line to Aquia Creek. The Alexandria and Fredericksburg Railway (which was now owned by the Pennsylvania Railroad) completed its line to a connection with the RF&P at Quantico on July 2, 1872. Through passenger service without change of cars could now be operated between Baltimore, Maryland and Weldon, North Carolina. The RF&P discontinued its steamboat operations between Quantico and Washington in favor of the all-rail route in 1877.

However, the increased rail traffic generated by the through service also increased the

The Byrd Street Station, located at the corner of Canal and 7th Streets, served as the passenger station and corporate office building for both the RF&P and the Richmond and Petersburg railroads. Opened on April 10, 1887, the Romanesque styled terminal had passenger waiting rooms, ticket office, restaurant, Pullman and Western Union offices, stationmaster's office, and train dispatcher's office on the first floor. The headquarters office for the railroads was located on the second floor. Adjoining the station was a freight terminal of the R&P RR and a yard for receipt and delivery of RF&P carload freight. Byrd Street Station was a stub-end facility with six stub-end tracks, each having a capacity for only six cars. Reverse movements were necessary to get trains in and out of the station and with the through trains often consisting of 16 to 18 cars, two cuts were necessary to get a train into the station. Delay and congestion resulted, especially when more than one train was in the station. Further, the train shed was located sideways to the station which necessitated that passengers cross tracks to get to and from trains. (William E. Griffin, Jr. Collection)

number of trains operated over the city streets in Richmond. To accommodate the city's objections, in 1875 the RF&P substituted horse power for steam locomotives to pull its trains on Broad Street east of Belvidere Street. It also erected a new shop facility at Boulton near the Belvidere connection. In 1880 the RF&P moved its train operations from Broad Street completely by building a new station in the vicinity of Broad and Pine Streets at its junction with the Connection Railroad. Known as Elba, this station continued in operation until 1919 and was widely used by the residents of Richmond's West End.

During this period, Baltimore produce merchant William E. Walters and his banking associate Benjamin F. Newcomer, acquired control of the Richmond and Petersburg Railroad, the Petersburg Railroad, the Wilmington and Weldon Railroad and a number of other railroads in the South, later consolidating them to form the Atlantic Coast Line Railroad. In 1885, control of the RF&P also passed to Walters and Newcomer when they purchased a large block of the company's stock from the RF&P's Philadelphia stockholders. In 1887 the RF&P and the Richmond & Petersburg Railroad built a new passenger station at the corner of Byrd and 7th streets in Richmond as a joint facility for the two railroads. The new Byrd Street Station also provided space for the general offices of the two companies. In 1888, the RF&P participated in the new "*New York and Florida Special*", a Pullman passenger train that ran three times a week between New York and Jacksonville. The RF&P also participated in the new through fast freight service known as the "*Atlantic Coast Dispatch*", established to move fresh fruits and vegetables in train loads from the south to the northern markets. Much to the displeasure of city, all of these trains moved over the streets of Richmond.

To avoid a confrontation with the city and to provide for the better operation of through trains, in November of 1888 the RF&P and the R&P RR agreed to jointly construct a belt line from Branch's Crossing (now Acca) on the RF&P to Clopton on the R&P RR to accommodate the freight trains then operating on the Connection Railroad. This belt line, known as the James River Branch, skirted to the west of Richmond and to the west and south of Manchester. The RF&P was the ACL's direct link to the Northern markets and had it not been for the entry of the Seaboard Air Line Railway it is possible that the RF&P might eventually have been absorbed into the ACL system. However, everything changed in 1900 when the SAL extended its line to Richmond.

On January 1, 1924, a large and modern locomotive terminal was opened by the RF&P on property immediately west of the railroad's Acca freight yard. Known as the Acca Locomotive Terminal, the facility consisted of a 30-stall roundhouse, machine shop, rest and locker building, office building, heating plant, coaling station and steam engine inspection pits on a 160-acre tract. Machine, boiler, blacksmith and erecting shops were later moved to Acca from Boulton and by 1937 all locomotive work had been consolidated at the facility to perform services on RF&P locomotives and road locomotives of the ACL. The coal station, shown in this photo, was a reinforced concrete structure with a capacity for 1,000 tons of coal. There were two storage bins, one which held 2/3 of the total storage and was used to supply RF&P locomotives. The other bin served the locomotives of the ACL. Both bins were equipped with two 15-ton weigh hoppers to record the exact amount of coal supplied to each locomotive tender. Beyond the coal tipple are the engine inspection pits, ash pits and ash pit crane. To the right is the ground storage facility. (William E. Griffin, Jr. Collection)

RF&P Pacific type 4-6-2 No. 401 charges around the "Eastern View Curve" at Mile Post 54, south of Fredericksburg on July 2, 1946 with a southbound freight train of 48 cars. Originally numbered No. 1, the 401 was one of six heavy dual-purpose 4-6-2's built for the RF&P by Baldwin in 1915-16. Nos. 1-6 were used in heavy freight and fast freight service for many years and in 1926 were renumbered 401-406. During that period an Elesco Feedwater Heater was installed and the air pumps were moved to the upper front portion of the smokebox. The locomotive's tender held 15 tons of coal and 10,000 gallons of water which was frequently supplemented by the addition of an auxiliary water tank as shown in this photo. (William E. Griffin, Jr. Collection)

The SAL had been assembled over a five year period between 1895 and 1900. During that period, Richmond banker John Skelton Williams and his associates purchased the control of a number of separately organized railroads that operated through six Southeastern states from Virginia to Florida. It was Williams' desire to bring the SAL to Richmond, and possibly Washington, if arrangements could not be reached with the RF&P to handle SAL's through traffic. At first, the ACL-controlled management of the RF&P refused to work out satisfactory arrangements to handle the SAL traffic. However, both the ACL and RF&P underestimated Williams' political influence in the Commonwealth. When the General Assembly of Virginia passed an act on March 3, 1900 granting John Skelton Williams a charter to build a new railroad between Richmond and Washington and coupled to this franchise the condition that the incorporators of the new railroad could purchase the Commonwealth's interest in the RF&P's common stock, the RF&P and its controlling interests quickly acquiesced in agreement for the interchange with SAL at Richmond. This agreement provided that the facilities of the RF&P would be enlarged and that SAL traffic would be handled by the RF&P on the same terms and conditions applied to the traffic of the ACL. This agreement also resulted in major changes in the ownership and operation of the RF&P.

To ensure the RF&P's commitment to handle the SAL's traffic on the same terms and conditions as that of the ACL required that the control of the RF&P be removed from the ACL and divided equally among the various connecting lines. On July 31, 1901, an agreement was reached between the Pennsylvania Railroad, Southern Railway, Chesapeake and Ohio Railway, Baltimore and Ohio Railroad, ACL and SAL to create a proprietary company, the stock of which would be held one-sixth by each of the parties to the agreement. This new company would be known as the "Richmond-Washington Company." The Richmond-Washington Company acquired all of the stock of the Pennsylvania Railroad controlled Washington Southern Railway (which had been formed on April 10, 1890 by merger of the Alexandria and Washington Railway and the Alexandria and Fredericksburg Railway) and the majority of the voting stock of the RF&P. Thereafter, the RF&P was controlled by the Richmond-Washington Company, a holding company, through ownership of a majority of the outstanding voting

Similar in appearance to the 400-series 4-6-2's were the 300-series 4-6-2's used by the RF&P in fast passenger service. Originally numbered 10-21, they were built for the RF&P by American Locomotive Company's Richmond Works and Baldwin Locomotive Works between 1918 and 1925. They were renumbered 301 to 312 and could handle scheduled runs between Richmond and Washington with as many as 14 heavyweight Pullmans northbound and 12 southbound. After the arrival of the 4-8-4 "Governors" and "Statesmen", these locomotives were used in local passenger service. Pacific No. 311 leads southbound local passenger train No. 23 across the Little River Bridge at Taylorsville on November 7, 1948. Note the three 840-series streamlined coaches originally purchased for use on the Old Dominion *that have been reassigned to the consist of No. 23's train. (August A. Thieme, Jr. Photo/William E. Griffn, Jr. Collection)*

capital stock. The Commonwealth of Virginia retained one-sixth ownership of the voting capital stock and the statutory right to appoint two of the company's directors. The remaining stock was in the hands of the public. In 1901, the operation of the Washington Southern was taken over by the RF&P and thereafter the two railroads were operated as one unit. The Washington Southern was merged into the RF&P on February 24, 1920.

The plans to upgrade the Richmond-Washington Line included the construction of a new passenger station just west of the Alexandria city limits to be used jointly by the C&O, Southern and Washington Southern and the construction of extensive facilities between Alexandria and the Long Bridge to be known as "Potomac Yard." This facility would serve as the major clearinghouse for the freight traffic of the Pennsylvania and B&O railroads on the north and C&O, Southern and Washington Southern railroads on the south. The six interested railroads adopted a plan of operation for Potomac Yard on December 5, 1905 and it was opened for service on August 1, 1906. The connection with the Southern Railway was established a mile south of Alexandria at "AF" Tower and both the Southern and C&O were granted trackage rights over the Washington Southern to Potomac Yard for freight traffic and to the Long Bridge for passenger traffic. At the same time, the B&O was granted trackage rights over the Pennsylvania between Anacostia Junction in Washington and the south end of the Long Bridge. The Southern Railway became dissatisfied with the operation of Potomac Yard and gave notice on September 1, 1924 that it would withdraw from the yard. It then began construction of its own terminal freight yard at Cameron Run. However, after further negotiations and a 1925 agreement providing for the handling of its traffic, the Southern reentered Potomac Yard on October 1, 1925. The original Potomac Yard agreement was superseded by a new agreement between the tenant roads in 1927. The railroads also entered into an agreement to organize the Washington Terminal Company for the purpose of building and operating a joint passenger facility to accommodate the passenger trains of all the tenant lines. The new union station was opened on November 17, 1907.

On the south end of the RF&P, agreements were reached to construct a new passenger terminal and to upgrade operations on the James River Branch. In 1916, the RF&P and the ACL reached an agreement to charter the Richmond Terminal Railway Company to erect and operate a new station on Broad Street. Construction began in 1917 and the magnificent new station was opened for service at noon on January 6, 1919. The RF&P also relocated its corporate offices from the First National Bank Building (which it had occupied since 1912) to its new quarters in Broad Street Station in December of 1918. Other provisions of the agreement provided for the rebuilding and double tracking of the James River Branch; operation by the ACL on the RF&P's line from Pier 5 of the James River Bridge to Acca Yard for freight service; enlargement of the RF&P locomotive facilities; and the use of the respective freight facilities of the RF&P and ACL for traffic of the other road. With the abandonment of operations on the Connection Railroad and the depression of the double tracks on the James River Branch to eliminate grade crossings, the RF&P was finally able to completely remove all train operations from the streets of Richmond.

Five years later, in 1924, a modern steam locomotive terminal was put in service at Richmond's Acca Yard. Located adjacent to the freight yard, the Acca Locomotive Terminal serviced and maintained the steam locomotives of the RF&P. It also serviced and performed running repairs on the road locomotives of the ACL. Only the passenger car shop and offices of the mechanical department remained at the old Boulton location. In 1927, automatic train control and cab signals were installed on all RF&P road locomotives. This safety feature included a device in the locomotive cab which showed the signal indications corresponding to those on wayside signals along the line as well as another device that automatically slowed down or stopped a train if it exceeded a given speed limit.

The Second World War provided a thorough test of railroading ability throughout the nation as passenger and freight volume hit new highs. Beginning late in 1941 the withdrawal of all Atlantic coastal steamship service, because of German submarines and the government's requirement of the ships for military purposes, threw to the railroads, and particularly the RF&P, an enormous tonnage of freight which otherwise would have moved entirely by water. In 1943 RF&P traffic and revenue records were set as more than 8½ million passengers and more than 14 million tons of freight were carried. The daily average of trains operated was 103 (the equivalent to a train every 14 minutes) of which 57 were in passenger service and 46 in freight service. On April 21st of that year a maximum of 131 trains were operated. On April 23rd some 33,324 passengers were carried, the most in a single day during the railroad's history.

The RF&P was able to meet the demands of the war years as a result of its acquisition during the late-1930's of a group of modern steam locomotives. The 4-8-4 "Generals" were acquired for fast freight service in 1937 followed by the

In 1927 Baldwin delivered four of the largest Pacific 4-6-2 type locomotives ever owned by the RF&P. Numbered 325-327, the locomotives were the most powerful locomotives in passenger service on the RF&P prior to the delivery of the 4-8-4's. They could handle the scheduled runs with 16 Pullmans northbound and 14 southbound. The locomotives could also be used in fast freight service and here we see No. 326 passing the Alexandria passenger station en-route to Potomac Yard in 1943 with a northbound perishable train. With the arrival of the new 4-8-4's, the RF&P sold these locomotives to the C&O in 1947. (Homer R. Hill Photo/Willam E. Griffin, Jr. Collection)

As the country was recovering from the Great Depression, the RF&P was faced with the demand for motive power that could handle heavier trains, both passenger and freight, on faster schedules. That demand was met by a fleet of twenty-seven 4-8-4 type steam locomotives that were named for Confederate Generals and Virginia Governors and Statesmen. Delivered in 1937, the Generals were numbered in the series 551-555. Particular attention was paid to the appearance of the "Generals" so as to make them look unusually attractive and modern. In this photo we see No. 553, the "General J. E. B. Stuart" in a builder's photo at the Baldwin Locomotive Works at Eddystone, Pennsylvania. (William E. Griffin, Jr. Collection)

4-8-4 "Governors" and later "Statesmen" that could be operated in both fast passenger and freight service. The "Generals" were named for generals of the Confederacy, the "Governors" were named for famous governors of the Commonwealth, and the "Statesmen" for famous statesmen from the Old Dominion. The RF&P's first diesels, two 1000-horsepower diesel-electric switch engines, were placed in service in March of 1942 at Acca Yard. Diesel switchers were first placed in service at Potomac Yard in August of 1944. The RF&P began its transition from steam to diesel road power in 1949 with the purchase of 30 diesel locomotives for freight and passenger service. The change was completed with the operation of the last steam locomotive in 1953.

The decade of the 1960's marked the beginning of momentous change for the RF&P. With perennial decreases in its passenger service throughout the decade, the company finally ended its long history in the passenger business on May 1, 1971 when the National Railroad Passenger Corporation (Amtrak) assumed responsibility for the operation of passenger service over the RF&P and on most of the other remaining rail passenger routes throughout the country. It was also during the 1960's that the RF&P began to make substantial investments in the acquisition of land for development as commercial or industrial sites. In the years ahead the real estate activities would be an increasingly significant contributor to the company's earnings. A notable improvement to RF&P facilities during the 1960's was the construction of a new consolidated shop in Richmond. Known as Bryan Park Terminal, this facility housed the railroad's mechanical, engineering, purchasing and stores departments. The new facility was completed in 1962 on land once occupied by the Acca Locomotive Terminal. Removal of the old steam locomotive terminal provided land for the new consolidated shop and also provided additional land for industrial development. In 1964, the RF&P also acquired the Dahlgren Railroad line that had been put up for sale by the federal government. This line had been built during World War II to serve the old Naval Proving Grounds at Dahlgren and had been idle for about seven years. The RF&P refurbished a portion of the line and promoted industrial development along the adjacent trackage.

Significant changes also began to occur during the 1960's on the RF&P's owner and connecting lines. On December 31, 1962, the C&O acquired control of the B&O and five years later, in 1967, the SAL and ACL merged to form the Seaboard Coast Line Railroad. Within ten years, the Chessie System Railroads would be adopted as the new corporate identity for what had previously been the B&O, C&O and Western Maryland railroads. The Seaboard System railroad was formed through the consolidation of the SCL, L&N, Clinchfield and Georgia railroads. As a result of these mergers, the ownership interest of the B&O and C&O in the RF&P was transferred to the Chessie System. Similarly, the ownership of the ACL and SAL in the

No. 553, the "General J.E.B. Stuart" passes GN Tower at Greendale as it approaches Acca Yard in Richmond with a southbound freight on July 7, 1950 (D. Wallace Johnson Photo, William E. Griffin, Jr. Collection)

RF&P was transferred to the Seaboard Coast Line Inc. The 113-mile RF&P connected the Chessie System on the north with the Seaboard System on the south. In 1969, the former SAL's Hermitage yard in Richmond was closed and all of the functions previously performed at that yard were moved to RF&P's Acca Yard, which was being jointly used by the RF&P and SCL.

Another significant change in the RF&P's ownership occurred as a result of the Penn Central bankruptcy and the formation of the Consolidated Rail Corporation (Conrail). During this period the ownership of the Richmond-Washington Company's stock by the former Pennsylvania Railroad came to an end. Hence, by the late-1970's the capital stock of the Richmond-Washington Company was owned by the Chessie System Railroad, Seaboard Coast Line Industries Inc, Southern Railway and the Commonwealth of Virginia. Interestingly, Conrail did not retain an ownership interest in the RF&P, but did remain a tenant of Potomac Yard and continued to be a major connection for RF&P traffic handled through the yard. As a result of the federal legislation that created Conrail, the Delaware and Hudson Railway gained access to Potomac yard via Conrail trackage.

However, the end was drawing near for both Potomac and the RF&P. On September 23, 1980, the Interstate Commerce Commission approved the application of the Chessie System, Inc. and Seaboad Coast Line Industries, Inc. to merge the two holding companies into a new holding company to be known as CSX Corporation. The former Chessie and SCL each owned 40 per cent of the Richmond-Washington Company, which in turn owned 65.9 per cent of the RF&P's voting stock. Hence, as a result of the Chessie-SCL Inc. merger, CSX gained control of 80 per cent of the common stock of the Richmond-Washington Company and received ICC approval to control the RF&P. However, the RF&P would continue to operate as a separate, independent railroad and retained its own management. This was due to the fact that while CSX controlled the voting stock of the RF&P by virtue of the ownership of a majority of the Richmond-Washington Company, CSX only owned approximately 43 per cent of all classes of outstanding RF&P stock. There remained a substantial minority stockholder interest in the RF&P including 20 per cent of the voting stock of Richmond-Washington Company still held by the Southern Railway. Another factor influencing the retention of RF&P's autonomous management was the Commonwealth of Virginia's continued interest in the railroad. The State owned nearly 20 per cent of the RF&P's stock which was held in the investment fund of the Virginia Supplemental Retirement System. Moreover, legislation passed by the Virginia General Assembly provided that the Virginia Supplemental Retirement System could sell its RF&P stock, but only back to the Commonwealth at its demand. Another act of the Virginia legislature required legislative approval of any merger of a transportation company in which the state owned stock. Hence, the

Commonwealth was in a position to block any attempt by CSX to gain full control of the RF&P.

The continued existence of Potomac Yard was impacted by the N&W and Southern merger that created the Norfolk Southern Corporation in 1982. This merger enabled Southern to divert traffic from Potomac Yard by effecting an interchange with Conrail at Hagerstown, Maryland either via its sister road, the N&W, or directly by obtaining trackage rights over N&W's line. Conrail had wanted to divert traffic from Potomac Yard to Hagerstown to avoid the operational restrictions and escalating charges imposed by Amtrak for Conrail's use of the Northeastern Corridor. The RF&P had attempted to enhance the operational efficiency and halt the decline in traffic handled through Potomac Yard with the retirement of the southbound hump and the installation of a computerized process controlled humping system over the northbound hump. However, when an agreement was reached between Norfolk Southern and Conrail in June of 1988 to provide for a diversion of their interchange traffic to Hagerstown, it doomed Potomac Yard. Shortly after the NS/Conrail diversion of traffic from Potomac Yard, CSX began to operate pre-blocked run-through trains that bypassed Potomac Yard. Within four years of the beginning of the NS/Conrail diversion of traffic to Hagerstown, the mighty expanse that was once Potomac Yard had disappeared.

Beginning in 1985, CSX and RF&P began to discuss methods of combining the two companies' operations. Finally, a merger agreement was proposed in 1990. However, this proposal was controversial and the merger agreement was mutually terminated. Within months of the failed merger attempt, a new proposal was initiated by the Virginia Retirement System. Under this proposal, VRS and CSX jointly proposed to RF&P a transaction in which CSX would acquire the RF&P's railroad operations in exchange for its share of RF&P stock and VRS would buy the remaining RF&P shares held by CSX. Upon the consummation of the transaction, the RF&P would become a real estate company, with VRS as its majority stockholder and only the railroad operations would be transferred to CSX. Following months of negotiations, the demise of the RF&P railroad was accomplished in a series of interrelated and inseparable transactions detailed in three agreements between the parties. The 157 year old RF&P would go out of the railroad business and become a real estate company controlled by the Virginia Retirement System. All of the RF&P's rail assets (except for the Potomac Yard real estate) were sold to RF&P Railway, a wholly owned subsidiary of CSX. Within a year, RF&P Railway was merged into CSX and it went out of existence. On the morning of October 10, 1991, the long and proud history of the RF&P Railroad came to an end.

Since the Generals were confined to freight service, the RF&P purchased a second group of 4-8-4 locomotives from Baldwin in 1938. These new locomotives were similar in design to the Generals except that they were slightly lighter and had several refinements to make them suitable for high speed passenger service. Unlike the Generals and the later Statesmen, the Governors were equipped with Vanderbilt style tenders. Their road numbers were 601-606 and since each bore the name of a former Virginia Governor, they became known as the "Governors". They performed so well that six identical locomotives (numbered 607-612 and also named for governors) were ordered from Baldwin in 1941. Here 4-8-4 No. 602, the "Governor Thomas Jefferson", waits at Broad Street Station for the arrival of an ACL train from the south and its next trip to Washington. The baggage handlers have already assembled the bags on their wagons to be loaded on the train upon its arrival. (Transportation Collections, Smithsonian Institution)

The Generals were restricted to freight service as they were too wide and heavy for operation across the Long Bridge and through the First Street Tunnel into Washington's Union Station. Here No. 551, the "General Robert E. Lee", passes between the Alexandria Passenger Station on the left and the old RF&P freight station on the right as it gets under way from Potomac Yard with a southbound freight train in 1947. (Herbert H. Harwood, Jr. Photo, William E. Griffin, Jr. Collection)

In 1945, Baldwin delivered the final order of 4-8-4 locomotives to the RF&P. These locomotives, numbered 613-622, were named for famous Virginia statesmen and unlike the "Governors", the ten "Statesmen" had large rectangular tenders and all axles on both the locomotive and tender were equipped with roller bearings. The "Statesmen" were the final steam locomotives purchased by the RF&P and were used in both passenger and freight service. Retired in 1953-54, several of the locomotives were retained for emergency service and then leased to the C&O for a brief period in 1955. "Statesman" No. 622, the "Carter Braxton" was the last RF&P steam locomotive to operate in regular service over the railroad. In this view we see "Statesman" No. 617 passing Virginia Avenue in Washington under PRR catenary with Train No. 92, the ACL's West Coast Champion in December of 1949. (Bruce D. Fales Photo, William E. Griffin, Jr. Collection)

RF&P southbound local passenger train No. 23 with 4-8-4 No. 608, the "Governor Henry A. Wise", passes Virginia Avenue Tower in Washington as it departs the tracks of Washington terminal and moves onto the tracks of the Pennsylvania Railroad in October of 1949. In only a few minutes, No. 23's seven car train will cross the Potomac River on the Long Bridge and enter the tracks of the RF&P. (E. L. Thompson Photo, Herbert H. Harwood, Jr. Collection)

In the early years of the Second World War the RF&P was required to lease steam locomotives from the C&O and Pennsylvania railroads to handle the increase in traffic over its line. The RF&P was able to terminate the lease of the foreign line locomotives in 1943 when it received ten powerful 2-8-4 locomotives from Lima Locomotive Works that had been ordered in 1942. Numbered in the series 571-580, these handsome Berkshire type locomotives had 69-inch drivers, exerted tractive effort of 64,100 lbs on 245-lbs boiler pressure and were designed exclusively for fast freight service. The 574 is shown near Acca with an extra freight soon after its delivery in 1943. (Anthony Dementi Photo, William E. Griffin, Jr. Collection)

RF&P 2-8-4 No. 572 rolls a northbound perishable train across the Rappahannock River Bridge at Fredericksburg with a clean stack in a late-1940's photo. The double track reinforced concrete arch bridge over the Rappahannock was designed by Mr. J. E. Greiner, who also designed the RF&P's bridge over the James River on the James River Branch at Richmond. The new bridge, elevated trackage and enlarged passenger station were part of a construction project begun in 1925 to improve operations at Fredericksburg. The first train operated over the new bridge on February 21, 1927. (Anthony Dementi Photo, William E. Griffin, Jr. Collection)

A track diagram of Potomac Yard and connecting lines. The enlarged detail of the yard (to the left in this drawing) shows the facilities located at the yard. (map by R. Wagner, William E. Griffin, Jr. Collection)

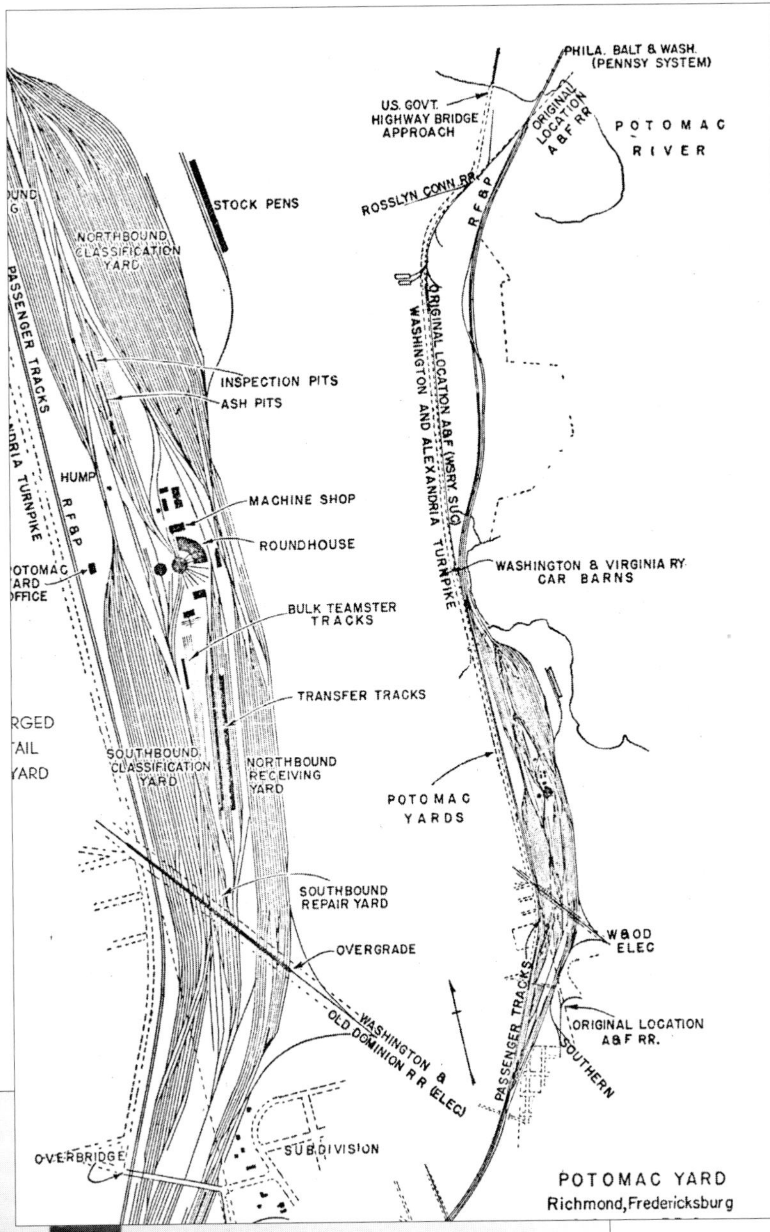

Two tracks in the northbound receiving yard could each accommodate 32 cars for re-icing. The Potomac yard ice house had a capacity of 130 tons per day with a storage capacity of 12,000 tons. Potomac Yard was discontinued as a regular re-icing station in August of 1967, the use of the facility having diminished with the disappearance of ice bunker type refrigerator cars. (William E. Griffin, Jr. Collection)

In 1943 the RF&P purchased three heavy mallet 2-8-8-2 type steam locomotives from the C&O for use in hump service. C&O Nos. 1558, 1564 and 1552 became RF&P Nos. 1, 2 and 3 respectively. They performed well as hump engines and had a tractive effort that was more than 40,000 lbs greater than the largest of the RF&P 0-8-0 yard switchers. Almost at the peak of the classification hump under a clear signal, 2-8-8-2 No. 2 shoves its cut of cars on a winter day in 1945. (Harry A. McBride, Jr. Photo, William E. Griffin, Jr. Collection)

Potomac Yard included an area of 520 acres. It was six miles long, 2,000 feet wide and contained 136 miles of tracks. Looking north over the shoulder of the car retarder operator, we see the northbound classification yard. In the distance is the Crystal City complex that was developed by the RF&P. Potomac Yard was the gateway, routing traffic coming to and from the great cities of the Northeast and South. (William E. Griffin, Jr. Collection)

The RF&P acquired its passenger diesels from the Electro-Motive Division of GM between 1949 and 1953. The RF&P owned fifteen E8 A-units numbered 1001-1015 and five E8 B-units numbered 1051-1055. Each unit was rated at 2,250-horsepower. The first service trip by an E8 on the RF&P was made by No. 1003 handling Train No. 14 northbound on December 2, 1949. In this view, Road Foreman of Engines Marvin Angel and the engineer are waiting for the conductor's signal for E8 No. 1011 to depart Broad Street Station with its northbound passenger train. (William E. Griffin, Jr. Collection)

The RF&P's first E8A diesel No. 1001 and one E8B unit pull Train No. 22, the northbound Silver Star *into Alexandria in 1964. (Jim Shaw Photo, William E. Griffn, Jr. Collection)*

The changing of the guard at Ivy City engine terminal in Washington, D.C. New F7A diesel No. 1101 is pictured beside 4-8-4 "Statesman" No. 622, the "Carter Braxton." To the left is one of the RF&P's 300-series 4-6-2 steam locomotives that worked local passenger assignments. Road diesel locomotives were placed in service on the RF&P in 1949. The "Carter Braxton" made the last regular service run on the RF&P. F7B units were equipped with steam generators so that F7A units, such as the 1101 pictured here, could be used in passenger service when operated together with a F7B unit. (H. B. McBride Photo)

The RF&P acquired eight F7A and eight F7B 1500-horsepower diesels from EMD in 1949. In 1950, it purchased two more F7A's and F7B's. The F7A's were numbered in the series 1101-1110 and the F7B's were numbered 1151-1160. An A-B-A set of F7's, led by No. 1104, speeds a perishable train over the well-maintained main line of the RF&P north of Richmond. (William E. Griffin, Jr. Collection)

F7A No. 1105 and two F7B units are north of Ashland with a northbound merchandise freight train. (William E. Griffin, Jr. Collection)

In July of 1962 the RF&P opened its new consolidated shop facility in Richmond. Known was Bryan Park Terminal, this shop housed the company's mechanical, engineering, purchasing and stores departments. The new consolidated shop allowed the RF&P to close the remaining operations at Boulton and bring all shop functions into one facility. (William E. Griffin, Jr. Collection)

A bevy of classic automobiles witness the southbound passage through Ashland of GP-7 No. 103 with the RF&P's south end local freight in May of 1962. The RF&P owned four EMD GP-7 diesels in the number series 101-104. (William E. Griffin, Jr. Collection)

Yes, Virginia's political capital–Richmond– was also Virginia's railroad capital. When railfans and people knowledgeable of railroading think of Virginia's foremost railroad city, the name of Roanoke comes instantly to mind. This is because Norfolk & Western had its headquarters there and in its shops built some of the best steam locomotives ever, and built them years after all other railroads had junked steam for diesels. But. . . Roanoke pales in a full comparison with Richmond.

In Richmond were the junctions of all of Virginia's major railroads except the Virginian. Albeit Norfolk & Western didn't come in directly, but had passenger service to and from Broad Street Station via the ACL to Petersburg, about 25 miles to the south. The great north-south trunk lines of the ACL and SAL had Richmond as their northern terminal, where they interchanged north-south traffic with RF&P. RF&P itself was the fast link between Richmond and Washington. C&O had three main lines radiating from Richmond. The Southern mainline didn't come near Richmond, but important secondary lines served the city. The city boasted many yards among these railroads. It had not one, but two monumental union stations: Main Street Station and Broad Street Station, as well as smaller passenger depots. Major LCL freight stations served all the roads, with attendant yards. The headquarters of the C&O and RF&P were in Richmond and in later years the SAL. Until 1927 the Richmond Works of the American Locomotive Company was the only locomotive builder in the South.

For these reasons it is quite justifiable to consider Richmond as the great hub of railroads in the Commonwealth, and also one of the great railroad hubs of the nation; gateway to the South.

The following pages show Richmond from the air in 1946. One can see how the railroads were all-pervasive in the city. Indeed, even today Richmond has a large and important railroad presence with the many lines of CSX and NS, and Amtrak has two stations.

Arguably the best known railroad landmark in Richmond is the famous Triple Crossing. Here a Southern Ry. industrial spur is crossed by the Seaboard Air Line's line into Main Street Station, and both are crossed by the C&O's James River Viaduct. This posed photo of the Triple Crossing is from about 1950. In this view, the C&O has a K-3a 2-8-2 with a westbound empty coal train on the top, while SAL is posing a brace of E7 diesels on a southbound train, and the Southern has a brand new Alco RS-2 on the bottom. This photo was taken by Dementi Studios of Richmond and used not only for a postcard (of the real photo variety), but by the publicity departments of the railways involved. (C&O Hist. Soc. Coll., COHS-29007)

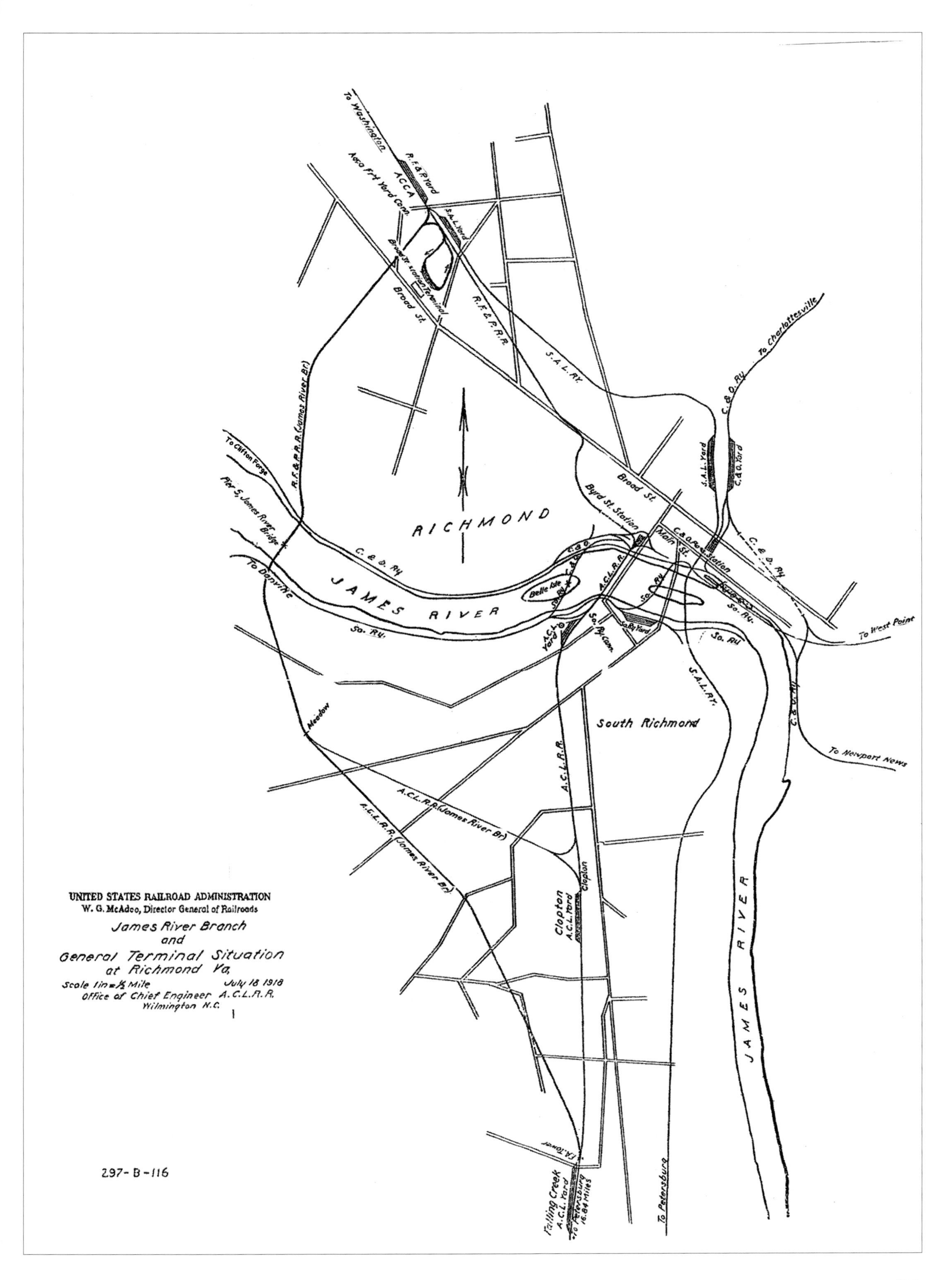
UNITED STATES RAILROAD ADMINISTRATION
W. G. McAdoo, Director General of Railroads
James River Branch
and
General Terminal Situation
at Richmond Va,
Scale 1 in = ½ Mile
July 18 1918
Office of Chief Engineer A.C.L.R.R.
Wilmington N.C.
297-B-116
RICHMOND
JAMES RIVER
South Richmond
Broad St.
Byrd St. Station
Main St.
Belle Isle
To Washington
To Charlottesville
To Clifton Forge
To Danville
To West Point
To Newport News
To Petersburg
Clopton
Falling Creek
Meadow

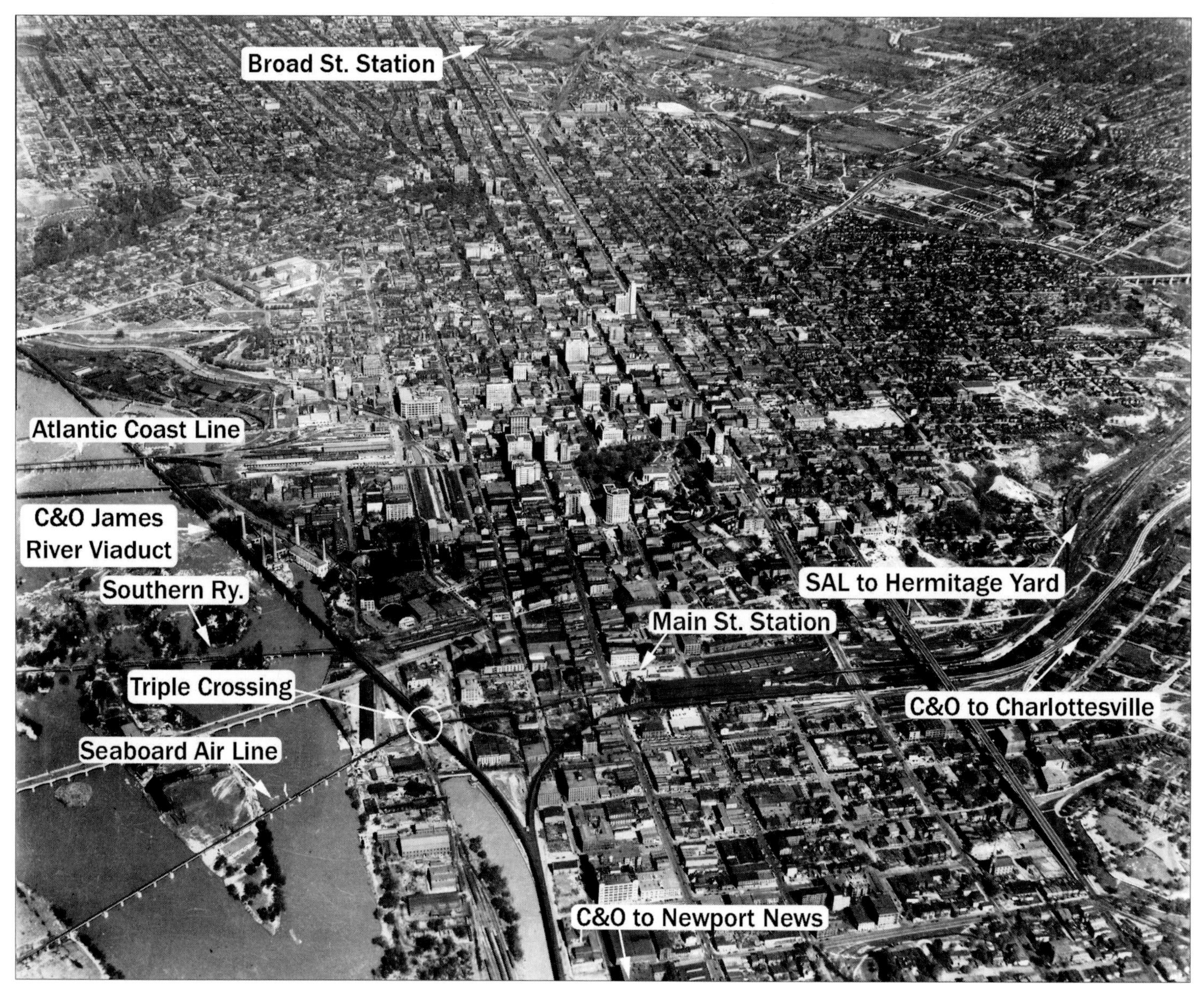

An aerial view looking north which shows the trackage and facilities of railroads in downtown Richmond. Visible is the Main Street Station facility, the famous triple crossing, the C&O viaduct and the numerous bridges across the James River into downtown Richmond. Broad Street Station is visible in the far distance.

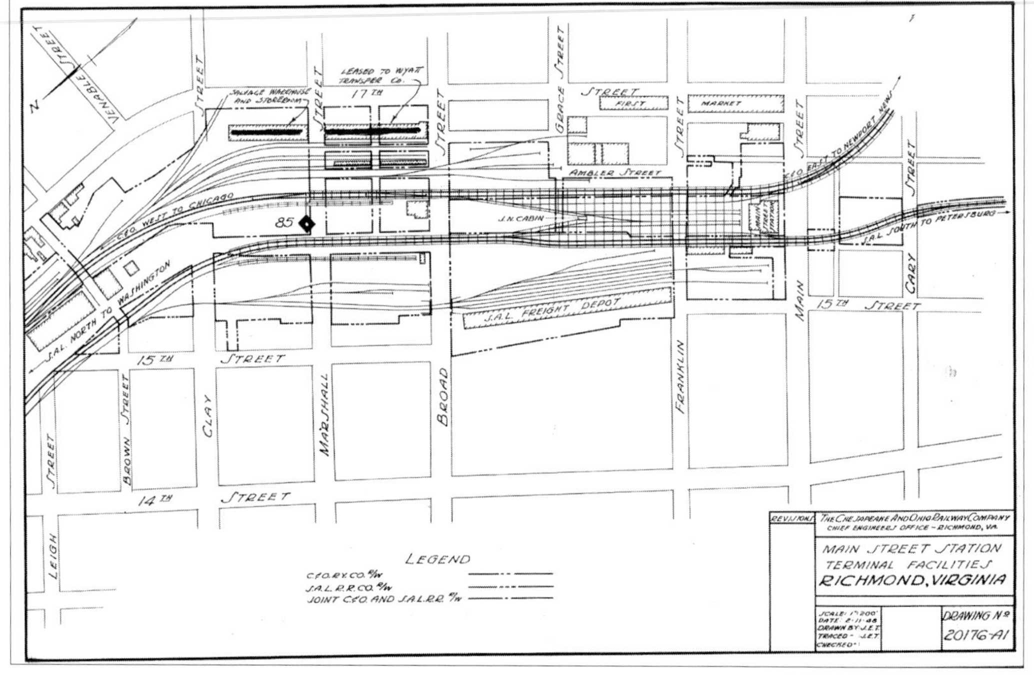

Track diagram of Main Street Station terminal facilities in 1948. (William E. Griffin, Jr. Collection)

Headhouse of the grand old Main Street Station in Richmond as it looked about 1950. The trackage on the west (left) side was used the Seaboard Air Line's north-south passenger trains, and the trackage on the east (right) side of the station was C&O's Piedmont Subdivision, were the Virginia sections of the name trains arrived and departed. The station was abandoned, partially burned, restored, used as office, and now has been beautifully restored and is again host to Amtrak trains using the C&O line to Newport News. This view is from the south-east, with Main Street passing right in front of the building, directly below the photographer.(C&O Ry. Photo, C&O Hist. Soc. Coll., COHS-29055)

Passengers in the Main Street Station waiting room (which was on the second floor) in 1946 could be waiting for either C&O's east-west trains (Newport News-Cincinnati) or Seaboard's north-south trains (Richmond-Florida). The windows open to the street side (south side) of the building and the train shed is behind the photographer. (TLC Collection)

In the early 1950s C&O renovated the Main Street Station's waiting room, placing a ticket office in the center and adding drop-lighting. Here a group of passengers awaits a train in August 1966. (C&O Hist. Soc. Coll., CSPR-11662.01)

Another distinctive feature of Main Street Station was its imposing train shed located at the north end of the building. Looking south in this circa 1956 overhead view we are able to see the C&O platform and tracks to the left and the SAL platform and tracks to the right. The elevated double tracks of the two railroads passed on the sides of the building and eight stub end tracks were used for storage of Pullmans and the mail cars that were terminated against the north end of the building between the viaducts. The train shed covered those stub end tracks. The white tower at the end of the platform and just north of the train shed is JN Tower. To the right in the photo, we see the SAL freight station that fronted on Franklin Street and handled LCL freight traffic. To the left of the station in this photo and fronting on Main Street on the east side of the station was the YMCA facility that provided lodging for away-from-home crews for many years. (C&O Historical Society Collection, COHS-29062)

On July 19, 1970, Train No. 42, the Virginia section of The George Washington, *lead by a single E8 diesel locomotive unit, pauses under the shed at Main Street Station. This view shows an unusual operation, eastbound. This view shows an unusual operation, as eastbound-trains usually ran on the outside track. (Thomas W. Dixon, Jr. photo, C&O Hist. Soc. Coll., COHS-30159)*

This view looks north from Main Street Station, which is behind us. The the left are the tracks of the SAL that passed on the west side of the station, and lead to SAL's Brown Street Yard. To the right are the tracks used by the C&O on the east side of the station, which lead to the C&O's 17th Street Yard and the Piedmont Subdivision line to Doswell and Charlottesville. (C&O Historical Society Collection)

An aerial view looking north from Main Street Station that shows the C&O line from the station through the 17th Street Yard to Charlottesville and the SAL line from the station through the Brown Street Yard to Hermitage.

The Richmond Terminal Railway was organized early in 1916 for the purpose of providing an improved and modern passenger terminal for the RF&P and ACL railroads. The project involved a new station, auxiliary buildings, a novel terminal track layout and an improved main line through the City of Richmond for passenger traffic to eliminate the many crossings at grade of important streets and the delays that were experienced at the Byrd Street Station. The station would also serve as the general office headquarters for the RF&P until 1976. Construction began in 1917 and the new Union Station of Richmond, or Broad Street Station as it was commonly known, was opened for business on January 6, 1919. Designed by New York city architect John Russell Pope, the terminal building is the perfect embodiment of the traditional classical style of architecture. Three stories high on plaza front, Broad Street Station was 246 feet long and 118 feet wide. The building faced Broad Street with an oval lawn between the street and the entrance roads to the right and left. A broad walkway led to the base of its portico which formed a colonnade of six massive unfluted columns with Doric capitals. Above the architrave was the station's most distinguishing feature - its dome. Set back from the street with a floor line about 8 feet above the street provided a commanding site for this monumental building. (William E. Griffn, Jr. Collection)

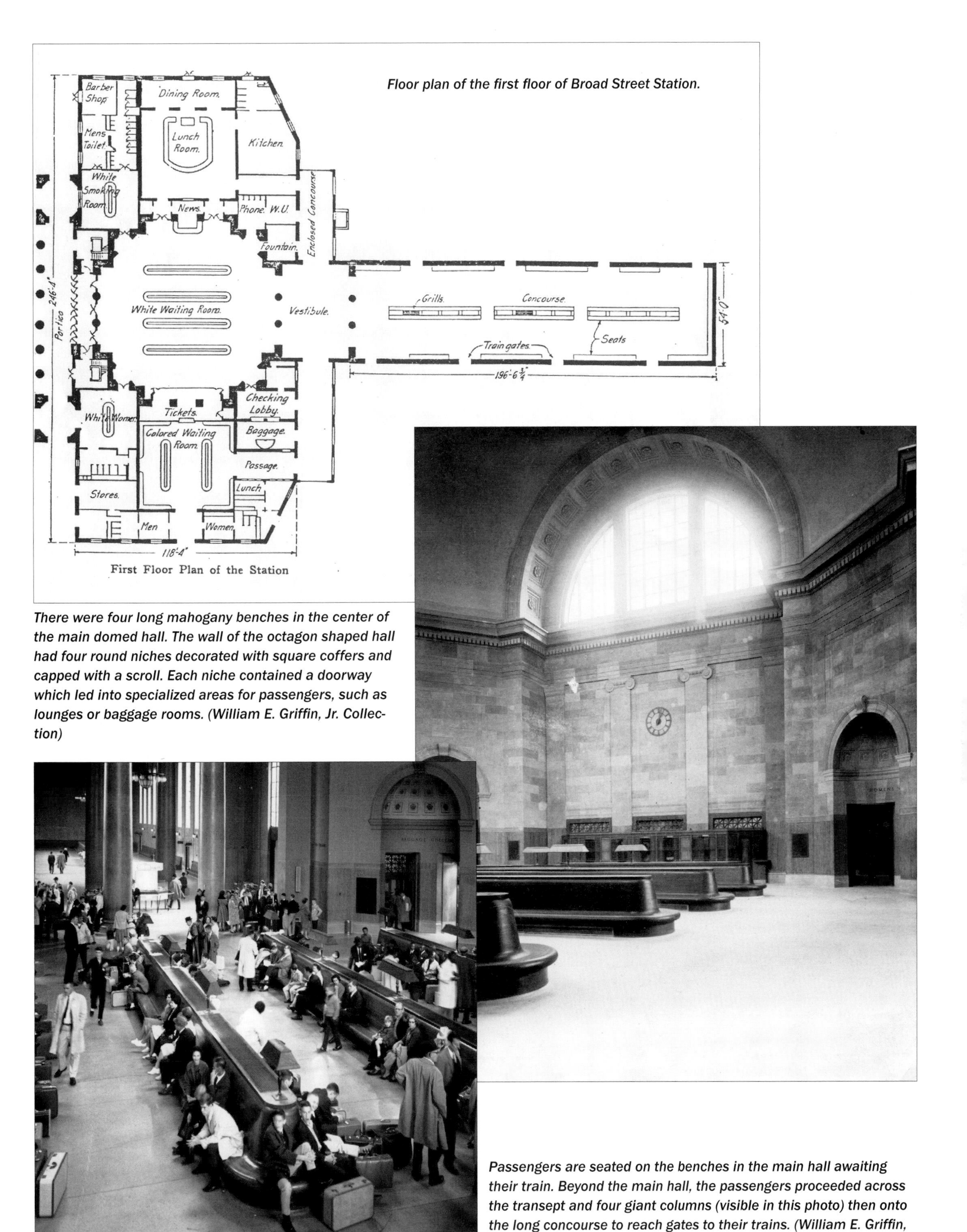

Floor plan of the first floor of Broad Street Station.

There were four long mahogany benches in the center of the main domed hall. The wall of the octagon shaped hall had four round niches decorated with square coffers and capped with a scroll. Each niche contained a doorway which led into specialized areas for passengers, such as lounges or baggage rooms. (William E. Griffin, Jr. Collection)

Passengers are seated on the benches in the main hall awaiting their train. Beyond the main hall, the passengers proceeded across the transept and four giant columns (visible in this photo) then onto the long concourse to reach gates to their trains. (William E. Griffin, Jr. Collection)

The track layout for Broad Street Station was unique. Designed by Harry Frazier, a consulting engineer for the City of Richmond, the tracks formed a loop so that both northbound and southbound trains entered the station headed in the same direction. This minimized switching and the interference of one train with another. It also allowed baggage, mail and express to be handled at one end of the platform, away from the portion of the platform used by the passengers. Northbound trains of the ACL approached the station over the James River Branch and the south leg of the Acca "wye", entering the station from the west by means of a second approach track leading off the RF&P's main line. All trains departed the station from the east, passing around the loop. Trains movements were controlled from two electro-pneumatic interlocking plants, one located at the "wye" connection (AY Tower) and the other at the station (JR Tower). (William E. Griffin, Jr. Collection)

An aerial view showing the facilities north-west of Broad Street Station, which is in the background to the south-east.

While it was the fourth largest rail system in the United States from the standpoint of mileage (over 10,000 miles in 13 states), the Pennsylvania Railroad ranked first in many categories. For the first two-thirds of the twentieth century, it was first among the nation's railroads in operating revenues and produced the greatest amount of freight tonnage. At the zenith of its existence, it also owned more locomotives, passenger cars and freight cars than any other line. From its origin in 1846 as a railroad chartered to build a line between Harrisburg and Pittsburgh, Pennsylvania, the railroad expanded between 1860 and 1890 by assimilating over 600 separate railroads into its system by purchase or long-term lease. Its position in the rail industry was so great that in 1916 the PRR adopted the motto that it was "The Standard Railroad of the World".

Following the War Between the States, the PRR decided to extend its expanding rail system into the South to match the ambitions of the Baltimore and Ohio Railroad. It organized the Baltimore and Potomac Railroad to parallel the Washington branch of the B&O and completed its line into Washington in the summer of 1872. By an Act of Congress on June 21, 1870, the Baltimore and Potomac RR was authorized to take over the Long Bridge over the Potomac River that had been built in 1808 by the Washington Bridge Company as a toll bridge for vehicular traffic. The PRR entered the Commonwealth of Virginia in 1872 when it acquired control of the Alexandria & Washington Railroad that had been operating from the south end of the Long Bridge to Alexandria since 1858. The PRR then rebuilt the Long Bridge to accommodate both vehicular and rail traffic. The PRR also took over the charter that had been granted to the Alexandria & Fredericksburg Railroad and began construction of that line from Alexandria to Quantico. The RF&P then extended its line to Quantico connecting with the line of A&F in 1872. In July of that year through train service wihout change of cars was inaugurated on a night schedule between Baltimore and Weldon, North Carolina.

In 1890, the Alexandria & Washington RR and the Alexandria & Fredericksburg RR were merged to form the Washington Southern Railway, which was controlled by the Pennsylvania RR. Following the completion of the Seaboard Air Line Railway into Richmond and the establishment of the Richmond-Washington Line in 1901 (discussed in the RF&P chapter of this book), the Pennsylvania RR relinquished all of its stock in the Washington Southern Railway. However, the Pennsylvania RR acquired one-sixth ownership in the Richmond-Washington Line and became a tenant in the new Potomac Yard that was opened in 1906 to handle the classification and interchange of freight traffic between the PRR and B&O railroads on the north and the C&O, Southern and Washington Southern railroads on the south. Potomac Yard would continue as the southern terminal for freight traffic of the PRR throughout the existence of the railroad.

The other rail line of the Pennsylvania RR in Virginia was on the Eastern Shore and it was linked to Norfolk via steamboats and barges that plied the Chesapeake Bay. Prior to the 1880's no rail line on the Delmarva Peninsula extended south of Pocomoke, Maryland. The southern end of the peninsula was an agricultural area with small towns and to be successful a rail-sea link

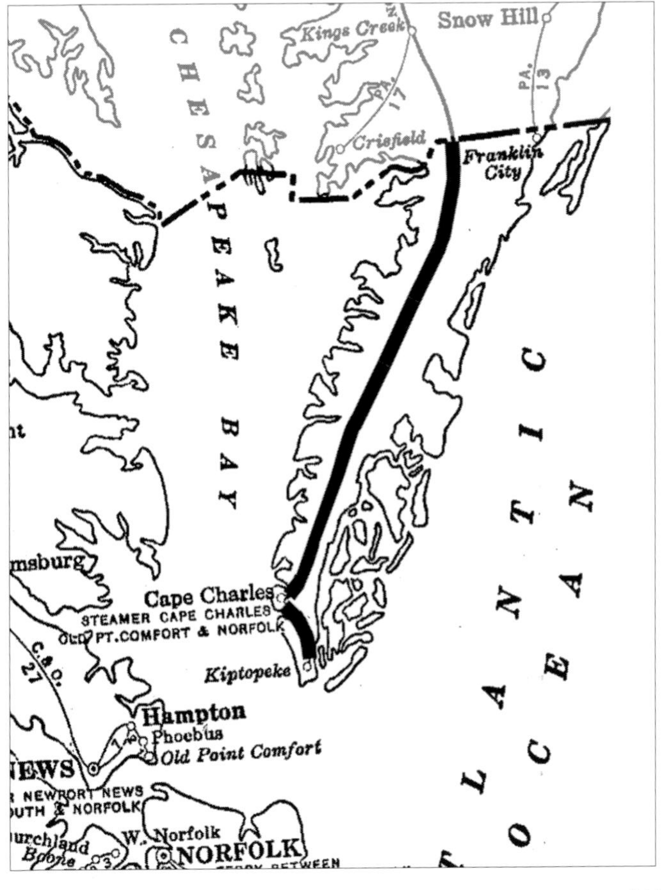

would be required across the bay to Norfolk. William A. Scott, a Pennsylvania congressman, and Alexander Cassatt, a PRR Vice-President of Traffic, envisioned such an operation. In 1882, Cassatt resigned his position with PRR to work with Scott on the proposed railroad. They organized the New York, Pennsylvania and Norfolk Railroad to build a rail line from a connection with the Philadelphia, Wilmington and Baltimore Railroad down the Eastern Shore of Maryland and Virginia. In 1884, the town of Cape Charles was created to serve as the southern terminus of the railroad. A yard, wharf and ferry slips were built and in 1884 the first trains operated into Cape Charles and passengers were then ferried across the 36-mile crossing of the bay on steamboats. In 1885, the railroad began to ship freight across the bay on specially designed barges. At Norfolk the NYP&N RR constructed a wharf and passenger depot at the foot of Brooke Avenue. For many years this depot was jointly used by the NYP&N RR and the C&O Ry. In 1920 the PRR leased the NYP&N RR and operated the line as a part of its Delmarva Division. In 1929, the PRR built a new freight yard and ferry terminal at Little Creek and abandoned its facility at Port Norfolk. Passenger service across the bay ended in 1958 and when the Penn Central bankruptcy led to the creation of Conrail, the Eastern Shore and Norfolk lines were not included in the new Conrail system. Since the 1977, the former NYP&N RR has been operated by two short lines - first the Virginia & Maryland Railroad and then the Eastern Shore Railroad.

The Pennsylvania Railroad extended the electrification of its line into Potomac Yard in 1935. Here we see No. 4834, one of the famous PRR GG1 class electics between runs at Potomac Yard on January 14, 1962. The PRR owned 140 of the GG1's that were built by GE and at the railroad's Altoona shops between 1934 and 1943. These electic motors had a continuous rating of 4,620 horsepower and were geared for a speed of 100 miles per hour. They were operated in both passenger and freight service on the PRR's Northeast corridor. (Jay Williams Collection)

Photographer Bruce Fales captured this splendid view of railroading on the Eastern Shore in the 1930's. Here we see Pennsylvania Railroad L1 class 2-8-2 passing semaphore signals as it rolls a freight train down the Delmarva Peninsula in 1936. (Bruce D. Fales Photo/Jay Williams Collection)

A Pennsylvania Railroad local freight rolls past RO Tower at the north end of Potomac Yard on a warm August 9, 1931. The locomotive is a L1 class 2-8-2 No. 1598. The PRR owned 574 of this class locomotive built by the railroad's Altoona shops, Baldwin and Lima between 1914 and 1919. The photographer - Bruce D. Fales - began taking photos of trains in 1920 and worked as a locomotive fireman for the B&O Railroad for many years, leaving in 1952 to work as a manager for the Washington Evening Star. While working in engine service, he took many photographs throughout the Northeast and northern Virginia. (Bruce D. Fales Photo/Jay Williams Collection)

This vintage postcard view shows the Pennsylvania Railroad facilities at Cape Charles, the terminus of that road's line down the Del-Mar-Va Peninsula. (TLC Collection)

The 277-mile mainline of the Clinchfield Railroad extended from Elkhorn City, Kentucky to Spartanburg, South Carolina touching five states and passing through some of the most rugged terrain in the Southeastern United States. Approximately 94 miles of the Clinchfield's main line were located in the Commonwealth of Virginia. From the south, the main line entered Virginia just north of Kingsport, Tennessee and passed through the southwest corner of the state exiting to the north in the vicinity of Elkhorn City.

While a railroad in the area served by the Clinchfield had been proposed since the early 1830's, the railroad was not built until after the turn of the century. In fact, it was the last Class I railroad built in the United States east of the Rocky Mountains. In 1908, the Carolina, Clinchfield and Ohio Railroad (CC&O) was incorporated to consolidate several short line railroads that had been built in the area. Extensions were then built north from Johnson City, Tennessee to Dante, Virginia and south to Bostic, North Carolina. The line was completed south to Spartanburg in 1909 and north to Elkhorn City in 1915. In 1924 the Atlantic Coast Line and Louisville & Nashville railroads jointly leased the CC&O and changed its name to the Clinchfield Railroad.

The most modern construction methods available at the time were utilized in the construction of the Clinchfield and even though it crossed a rugged section of two mountain ranges, track curvature was held to a maximum of 14 degrees and the grades never exceeded a maximum of 1.2 percent. To achieve this engineering feat required 55 tunnels and almost five miles of bridges and viaducts. A 7,854-foot tunnel was cut through Sandy Ridge, the Cumberland Mountains barrier between Virginia and Kentucky. At the Blue Ridge chain, a 4,135-foot tunnel was bored through Clinch Mountain. Of the 55 tunnels required on the line, 28 were located in the Commonwealth of Virginia. Tunnels represented 10 miles of the Clinchfield's main line. The five miles of bridges and viaducts that crossed seven divides between watersheds represented 3.5 percent of the total mileage. In all, more than 25 million cubic yards of earth and rock were moved in the construction of the railroad. However, the efforts of the engineers who designed and built the Clinchfield resulted in one of the best railroad road beds in the country with low grades and easy curvature.

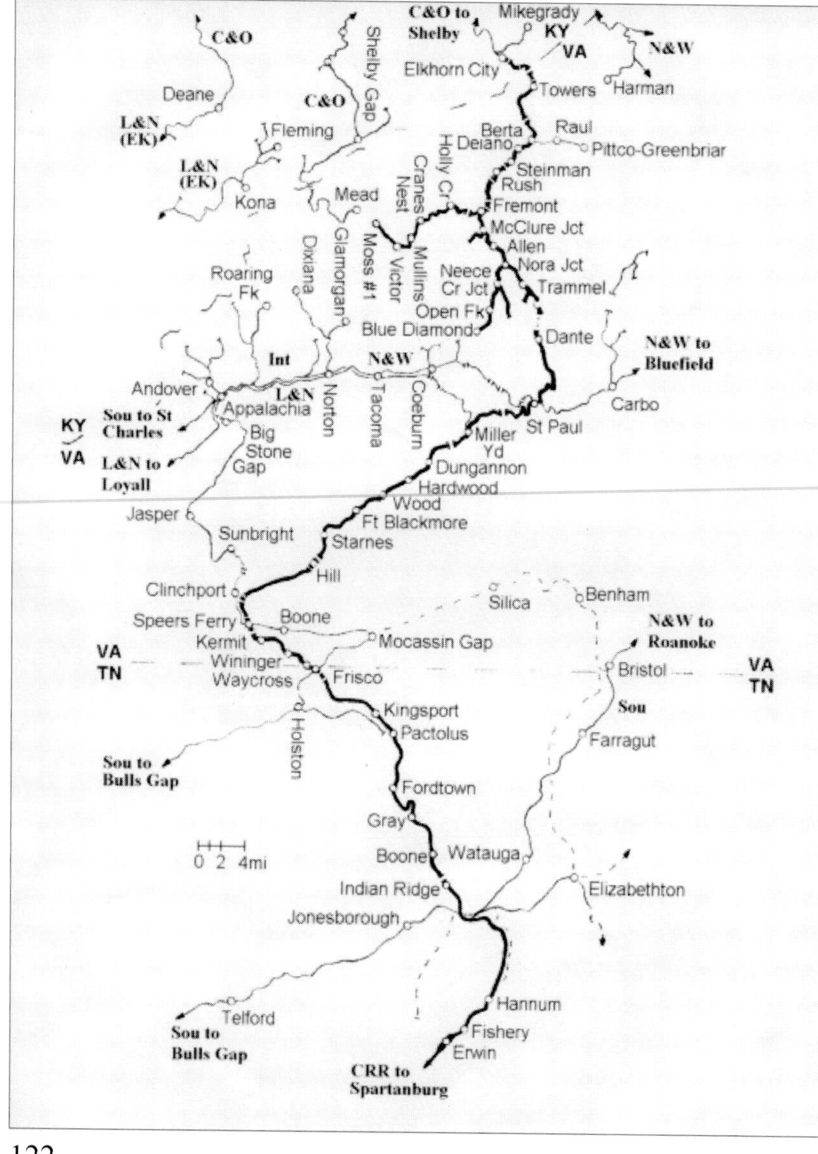

While the predecessor lines of the Clinchfield had been built to haul coal from the bituminous fields of southwestern Virginia - and coal did account for approximately half of all its tonnage - it also served as a true "bridge line" between the Atlantic seaboard and the Great Lakes. At Spartanburg it connected with the Southern Railway and the Atlantic Coast Line Railway-controlled Charleston and Western Carolina Rail-

To handle heavy traffic over its mountainous terrain the Clinchfield operated an unusually large number of articulated locomotives for the size of the railroad. The most notable of these locomotives were the E class 4-6-6-4, or "Challenger" type engine. The Clinchfield acquired twelve (Nos. 650-657, 660-663) of these locomotives new from the American Locomotive Works between 1942 and 1947. In 1947 it acquired six more "Challengers" (Nos. 670-675) secondhand from the Denver & Rio Grande Western Railroad. Here, E-1 class 4-6-6-4 No. 655 rolls south from Dante Yard with a coal train of the railroad's hopper cars. (B.F. Cutler Photo, C.K. Marsh, Jr. Collection)

way to Augusta, Georgia. The final section of the Clinchfield from Dante to Elkhorn City joined the line with the Chesapeake and Ohio Railway. This connection with the C&O allowed the Clinchfield to participate in the shipment of coal into the Ohio River valley and established the railroad's bridge route for coal and merchandise traffic between the Southeast and the Midwest.

In sharp contrast to its freight service, the Clinchfield offered only a modest passenger operation. Other than a convenient connection to the Southern Railway's passenger trains at Spartanburg, the Clinchfield could only offer a service that met the local needs of its sparsely populated operating territory. That service included an all-stop tri-weekly day train that required 11 hours in either direction between Elkhorn City and Spartanburg and a local day train between Erwin and Elkhorn City. The trains were powered by Pacific steam locomotives and were discontinued in 1955. The last passenger train was operated on May 2, 1955.

When the CC&O began operations in 1908, the company's equipment consisted of six steam locomotives and 269 freight cars. At the time of the ACL-L&N lease in 1925, the Clinchfield owned 96 locomotives and almost 8,000 freight cars. While the Clinchfield did roster some smaller freight and passenger engines of the Pacific and Mikado types, it used an unusually high percentage of Mallet, or articulated engines for the size of railroad. At the height of steam operations, sixty-five percent of its motive power consisted of locomotives of the 2-6-6-2, 2-8-8-2 and 4-6-6-4 wheel arrangements. The E class 4-6-6-4 locomotives in the number series 600 were considered to be the railroad's finest steam power.

The Clinchfield began to dieselize its motive power in December, 1948 when a group of ten new diesels arrived at Erwin. Complete dieselization of the road's power was accomplished in 1952. The Clinchfield's roster of diesels included yard switchers, road-switchers and cab units. All of the road's diesels were manufactured by the Electro-Motive Division of General Motors and were painted in a scheme of Confederate gray and yellow.

During the period of the ACL-L&N lease, the Clinchfield essentially operated as an independent line. The chairman of the board of both the ACL and L&N, and the respective presidents of those two roads served as a three-man executive board of the Clinchfield. A general manager served as the chief operating officer of Clinchfield and was stationed at the railroad's headquarters at Erwin, Tennessee. In 1971, the Seaboard Coast Line Railroad (which had been created by the merger of the ACL and SAL railroads) purchased all of the outstanding stock of the L&N Railroad. Following the acquistion of the L&N, the SCL formed the Family Lines System which was comprised of the SCL, L&N, Clinchfield, Georgia Railroad and the West Point Route and their subsidiary companies. The Family Lines System was not a formally merged entity but rather was an operating organization of associated companies and their leased and affiliated companies. Without going through the formal merger procedures required by the Interstate Commerce Commission, the member roads of the Family Lines were able to set traffic policies, solicit business and coordinate their operations, facilities, motive power and rolling stock. The separate identity of the Clinchfield ended in 1983 when it was merged into the Seaboard System Railroad.

Clinchfield Pacific type No. 153 with a short passenger train at Dungannon on May 30, 1952. (Bob's Photo / C.K. Marsh Collection)

USRA 2-8-8-2 heavy Mallet No. 731 has been turned, fueled, and serviced at Dante on June 28, 1947 and is ready to go out on another run. (Bob's Photo / C.K. Marsh Collection)

To cross a rugged section of the Smoky Mountains that reached a 2,629-foot summit and still hold the maximum grade to 1.5% required the construction of 55 tunnels on the Clinchfield totaling more than 10 miles in length. Twenty eight of those tunnels were located in the Commonwealth of Virginia, and here we see southbound Train No. 16 exiting the Stateline Tunnel in 1952. The lead locomotive is Clinchfield F7A No. 806, the first of 18 such diesels (806-823) owned by the railroad. When it came to Diesel locomotives, the Clinchfield was an all-EMD road with all of its motive power roster filled by that builder. (B.F. Cutler Photo, C.K. Marsh, Jr. Collection)

The Clinchfield's passenger service began in 1909 and ended in 1955. In the 1920's the railroad was operating two daily trains between Elkhorn City, Kentucky and Spartanburg, North Carolina. By the 1940's, the service was down to one coach train daily in each direction. The service was powered by a small fleet of 4-6-2, or Pacific, setam locomotives such as the one seen in this photo. Here we see Clinchfield Train No. 37 crossing the notable high trestle at Copper Creek in 1939. The Clinchfield on the high trestle, and the Southern Railway on the lower trestle, cross the confluence of Copper Creek and the Clinch River at this location in Scott County, Virginia. Both the Clinchfield and the Southern came south on the east bank of the Clinch River from the Clinchport area. (C.K. Marsh, Jr. Collection)

The Interstate Railroad is an 88 mile long primarily coal hauling railroad located in the Southwestern corner of the Commonwealth of Virginia. The company was incorporated in 1896 by the Virginia Coal & Iron Company and the following year five miles of rail line were built to connect the coal mines of the Stonega Coal & Coke Company with the Louisville and Nashville Railroad at Appalachia. During the early years the railroad owned only one locomotive and functioned solely as a mine run operation for the mines at Stonega and nearby towns.

Several branch lines were built by the Interstate as new coal mines were opened in the early 1900's. An important connection was established when the Virginia and Southwestern Railway (later acquired by the Southern Railway) was completed into Appalachia and granted the Interstate trackage rights over its line to Big Stone Gap. In 1909 the Interstate extended its line eastward to Norton where it made connection with the Norfolk and Western Railway.

The Interstate and the mines its served experienced their first real boom in business during the years of the First World War. Even though it was only a 25 mile long railroad at the time, its importance as an outlet for the region's coal was obvious to its owners. Following the war the Interstate was upgraded to the standards of the first class coal hauling railroads. A modern marshaling yard, car and locomotive shops, and a new general office building were built at Andover, near Appalachia.

In 1923 the Interstate extended its mainline another 18 miles to connect with the Carolina, Clinchfield & Ohio Railway (later the Clinchfield) at Miller Yard. This connection allowed the Interstate to become an important connecting link in the route of coal and merchandise traffic between the Midwest and the South via the L&N - Interstate - CC&O.

To handle the increased business over the line, the Interstate purchased two 2-8-8-2 mallet compound locomotives from the American Locomotive Works in 1923. The railroad's other motive power included heavy 2-8-0's, 0-6-0 switchers and Atlantic type passenger engines. Passenger service was never an important source of revenue for the Interstate and the service was discontinued in 1929. During and after the Second World War, the Interstate's motive power included three 2-6-6-2's acquired from the N&W, a 2-8-2 and two 2-8-0's from the Pennsylvania and four heavy 2-8-0's from the Southern. The Interstate dieselized its motive power in 1953 with a fleet of ten Alco RS-3 1600-horsepower locomotives. The diesels were painted in a distinctive orange and cream paint scheme. The roof and upper locomotive body, which were painted a cream color, were separated by a gray stripe from

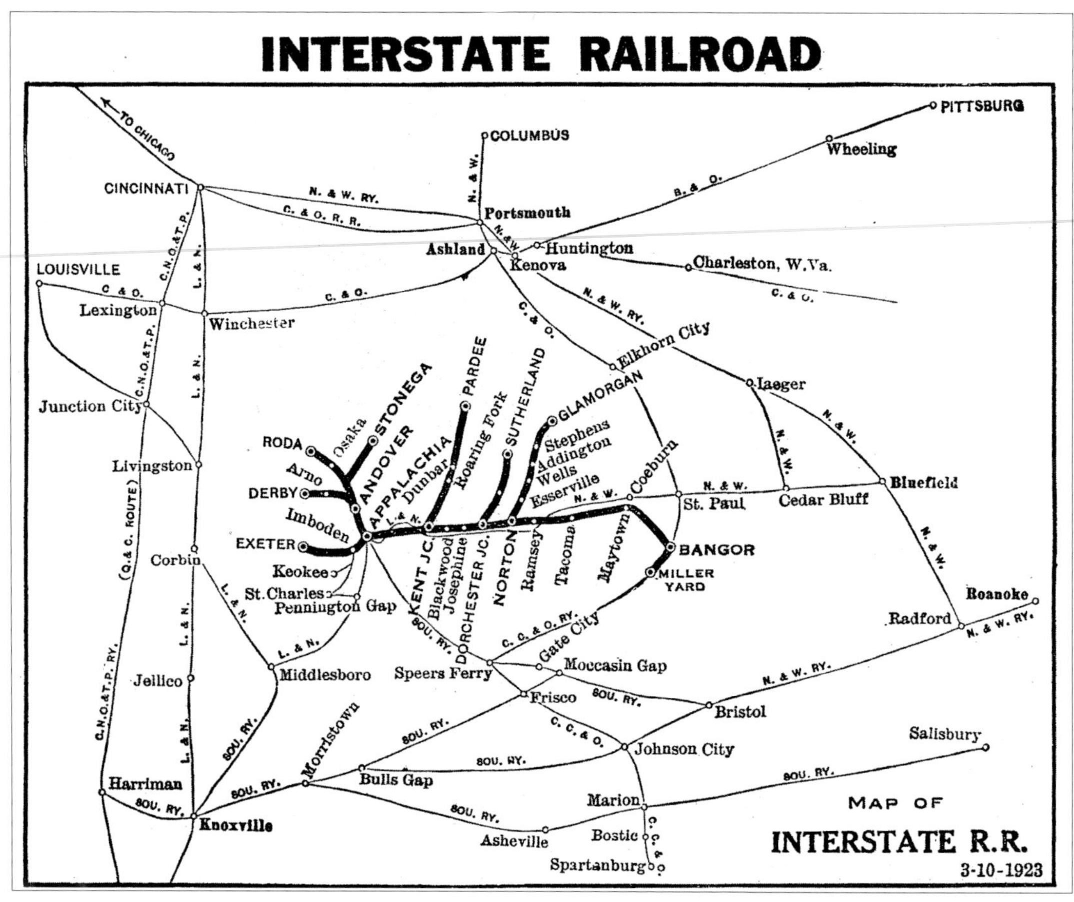

the orange lower body and cab. The locomotive numbers and lettering were painted black.

The Interstate owned an exceptionally large fleet of hopper cars for the size of its railroad. Solid trains of Interstate coal hoppers were routed over the N&W to Lamberts Point for export and over the Clinchfield to various locations in the South. In the post war years revenue from coal hauled and per diem from the operation of its fleet of hopper cars were offset by soaring operating costs. The Interstate was also hurt by a number of strikes by the coal miners that left the railroad with only a small amount of through merchandise traffic from its connections. In 1959, the Virginia Coal & Iron Company offered the Interstate for sale. Both the L&N and Southern bid for the road but it was acquired by the Southern in 1960. The Southern operated the Interstate as a wholly owned subsidiary.

In 1965, the Southern closed its yard at Appalachia and coordinated its operations with that of the Interstate at Andover. The Interstate's RS-3's were initially replaced by Southern F-units and later by new GP38's. The former Interstate locomotives were repainted in the Southern paint scheme at Atlanta and spent the remainder of their years working on assignments in Georgia and the Carolinas.

In 1982 the Interstate became a part of the new Norfolk Southern corporation created by the merger of the Southern and N&W railways. It ceased to exist as a separate corporate entity in 1985 when NS transferred control of the line to the Clinch Valley Extension of the Pocahontas Division.

Interstate Railroad coal hoppers are being loaded at the Wise Coal and Coke Company in Dorchester, Wise County, Virginia. Coal was discovered at Dorchester in 1880 and a typical coal camp was quickly established. The Wise Coal and Coke Company on the L&N Railroad at Dorchester was formed in 1902. The Sutherland Coal and Coke Company on the Interstate Railroad at Dorchester was formed in 1906. In 1917 they were consolidated to form the Wise Coal and Coke Company. The Interstate hauled coal, coke and timber from Dorchester Junction to the Southern at Appalachia, the N&W at Norton, the Clinchfield at Bangor (Miller Yard), and the L&N at Norton, Dorchester Junction and Appalachia. (Bob's Photo/TLC Collection)

Interstate 0-6-0 No. 10 was the second locomotive to be assigned that number by the railroad. It was built in 1918 by Baldwin as No. 11 but was reassigned as No. 10 when delivered to the railroad. It was one of three 0-6-0's owned by the Interstate and was photographed at Andover, Virginia on September 19, 1947. (L. M. Kelley Photo/TLC Collection)

Interstate 2-8-0 No. 6 is shown moving a coal train with three "headout" N&W hoppers near Appalachia, Virginia in July, 1949. The Interstate generally followed the valleys of the Guest River and Powell River to Appalachia and then along Callahan Creek to the main yard at Andover. (H. Reid Photo/William E. Griffin, Jr. Collection)

Interstate 2-8-2 No. 14 rolls past some well-worn cattle guards with a brisk exhaust as it hustles its train through the Powell River valley out of Andover, Virginia in July of 1949. No. 14 was one of two former Pennsylvania Railroad L-1 class Mikado type locomotives purchased second hand by the Interstate in 1948. (H. Reid Photo/William E. Griffin, Jr. Collection)

Again with "headout" N&W hoppers, Interstate 2-8-0 No. 28 moves a coal train near Norton, Virginia in 1952. No. 28 was one of four (Nos. 25-28) heavy Consolidation locomotives purchased from the Southern Railway in 1952. The remarkably clean locomotive is shown in service shortly after receipt from the Southern. (H. Reid Photo/ William E. Griffin, Jr. Collection)

The Louisville and Nashville Railroad was originally chartered in the Commonwealth of Kentucky to build a railroad between Louisville, Kentucky and Nashville, Tennessee. Without a change in its name, the railroad was expanded into a system of over 4,700 miles serving 13 states. Coal provided nearly half of the L&N's tonnage and over 30 per cent of all of its freight revenue. It was coal that eventually brought the rail lines of the L&N into the Commonwealth of Virginia. Expansion by acquisition, lease and construction enabled the L&N to gain access to the coal fields of Kentucky and in 1886 it began the construction of a branch line from Corbin, Kentucky to reach the rich coal and iron ore reserves in eastern Kentucky and western Virginia. A branch line, that would become the railroad's Cumberland Valley Division, dipped into Tennessee to cross the Big Stone Gap and then turned north into Virginia reaching Norton in 1891. The town of Norton was named for Eckstein Norton who was the president of the L&N at that time. The Cumberland Valley Division and the L&N's EK Division (EK for eastern Kentucky) provided an enormous amount of coal traffic for the L&N. This sole line of the L&N in Virginia, entered the Commonwealth just north of Cumberland Gap, Tennessee, at the extreme western tip of the state. It extended for approximately 57 miles to Andover, then through Appalachia and Dorchester Junction for about 15 miles to reach Norton, establishing important connections with the Southern, Interstate and N&W railroads at those locations.

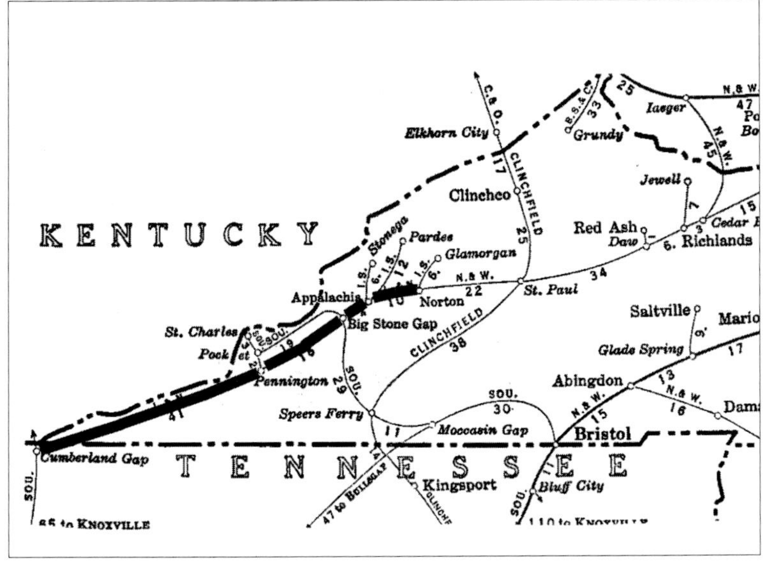

Far from the railroad's main line, this Louisville and Nashville passenger train is a making station stop at Norton, Virginia on August 17, 1937. Motive power is provided by one of the L&N's handsome K-2 class Pacifics No. 192. The L&N owned numerous Pacific, or 4-6-2 type steam locomotives in the classes K-1 through K-7. Light Pacifics like the 192, that was built in 1909, were assigned to branch line service. One of the L&N light Pacifics - No. 152 - survives today and is operated by the Kentucky Railway Museum at New Haven, Kentucky. (TLC Collection)

Chartered in 1827, the Baltimore & Ohio Railroad began operation on 13 miles of line between Baltimore and Ellicott Mills, Maryland in 1830. It was the first common carrier railroad in America and the first to offer scheduled passenger and freight service to the public. By 1900, the B&O was a rail system of over 6,000 miles in 13 states that connected Chicago and St. Louis to Baltimore, Washington, Philadelphia and New York.

The only significant B&O trackage in Virginia was represented by two lines that operated between Harpers Ferry, West Virginia and Strasburg, Virginia. The Winchester and Potomac Railroad was chartered in Virginia in 1831 to build a rail line from Winchester to a junction with the B&O at Harpers Ferry. The B&O was completed to Harpers Ferry in 1834 and the two railroads were joined on the Virginia side of the river when a bridge across the Potomac was completed in 1837. This connection caused Virginians great concern for lost of business to Baltimore and the Virginia state legislature would not authorize further construction by the W&P south of Winchester. This situation would change after the War Between the States. In 1867, the W&P was leased to the B&O and the Winchester and Strasburg Railroad, under the control of the B&O, was chartered to build a rail line between its namesake cities. This line was opened in 1870 and provided for a direct line controlled by the B&O from Harpers Ferry to Strasburg. The B&O then leased the Virginia Midland's Harrisonburg Branch from Strasburg to Harrisonburg and proceeded to build its own rail line from Harrisonburg to Lexington. However, when the B&O was driven into bankruptcy as a result of the cost of constructing the Howard Street Tunnel and defaulted on its lease payments to the Southern, the SRR resumed control of the Harrisonburg Branch from Strasburg to Harrisonburg in 1896. The portion of the line between Harpers Ferry and Strasburg and from Harrisonburg to Lexington remained under B&O control. The portion between Harpers Ferry and Strasburg became the B&O's Shenandoah Sub-Division and the portion of the line between Harrisonburg and Lexington became the B&O's Valley Division until sold in 1943 to the Chesapeake Western Railway.

Baltimore and Ohio Train No. 55, the "Valley Local", makes a station stop at the Winchester station on October 26, 1946. Even after the Strasburg to Harrisonburg portion of the Harrisonburg Branch was returned to the Southern Railway, the B&O operated its trains from Harpers Ferry to Strasburg and from Harrisonburg to Lexington. For a period of time it was possible to take through trains from either Baltimore or Washington to Harrisonburg or Lexington. B&O trains from Baltimore or Harpers Ferry changed engines at Strasburg from B&O to Southern power and then changed to B&O again when the train reached Harrisonburg for the remainder of the trip to Lexington. (William E. Griffin, Jr. Collection)

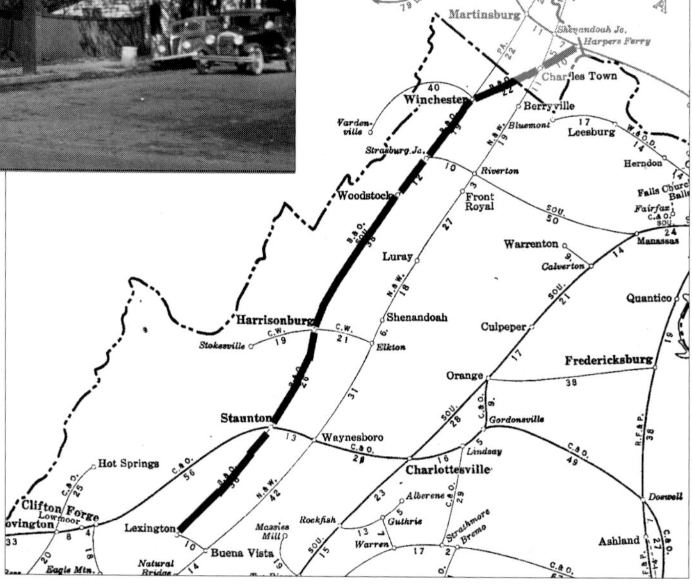

The original Norfolk Southern Railway (not today's vast Norfolk Southern Corporation) operated a main line that extended south and west from Norfolk, Virginia into the state of North Carolina. While the majority of its trackage was located in North Carolina, there were four separate lines of NS trackage in the Commonwealth of Virginia. During the steam era the NS divided its operations into Steam Divisions and Electric Divisions. Two of the Virginia lines were in steam divisions and two were in electric divisions.

One steam division line was the main line of the NS that extended south and west from Norfolk to Charlotte, North Carolina. Of the approximately 398 miles of main line between those locations, only about 30 miles were located in Virginia. The Virginia portion of the main line was built by the Elizabeth City & Norfolk Railroad in 1881. The NS was also one of the proprietary owners of the Norfolk and Portsmouth Belt Line Railroad and interchanged traffic with the N&PBL at Berkley. The construction of VGN into Norfolk provided the NS with a more direct route into the city for its passenger trains. When the VGN was built into Norfolk, its line crossed the NS main line at Carolina Junction and the NS line to Virginia Beach at Tidewater Junction. The NS used the VGN trackage into Norfolk and beginning in 1912, the new Norfolk Terminal Station was opened to serve the passenger trains of NS, VGN and N&W. Electric division trains of the NS did not operate into Norfolk Terminal Station until 1917 when overhead trolley wires were completed into the station.

Another steam division line in Virginia was the NS line from Suffolk to Edenton, North Carolina, that was a part of the NS Suffolk & Carolina Division. This line of railroad was initially built in 1874 by the narrow gauge Suffolk and Carolina Railway for the purpose of hauling timber from the edge of the Dismal Swamp to saw mills in Suffolk. The 50-mile line from Suffolk was completed to a connection with the NS main line at Edenton in 1902. In 1906 the railroad was purchased by the Virginia and Carolina Coast Railroad, which was promptly merged into the NS the same year. Following the NS bankruptcy during the Great Depression, the line from Suffolk to Edenton was abandoned and its terminal properties in Suffolk were sold to the VGN in 1940.

The NS also operated two interesting routes on its Electric Divisions. The NS acquired the first line in 1900 when it purchased the Norfolk, Virginia Beach and Southern Railroad. This line was originally built in 1883 between Norfolk and Virginia Beach as a narrow gauge railroad and went through two reorganizations and rebuilding to standard gauge before acquired by the NS. It was considered to be the "South Shore" route and NS trains were initially powered by steam locomotives. In 1902 the Chesapeake Transit Company built a competing line from Norfolk to Virginia Beach via Cape Henry. This railroad was considered to be the "North Shore" route and was an electric traction standard gauge line. The NS then extended its steam operated line along the ocean at Virginia Beach to reach Cape Henry. For two years there were competing lines to the beach, but the public clearly preferred the electric operation and in 1904 the NS electrified its "South Route" as far as Virginia Beach and abandoned the steam operated line from Virginia

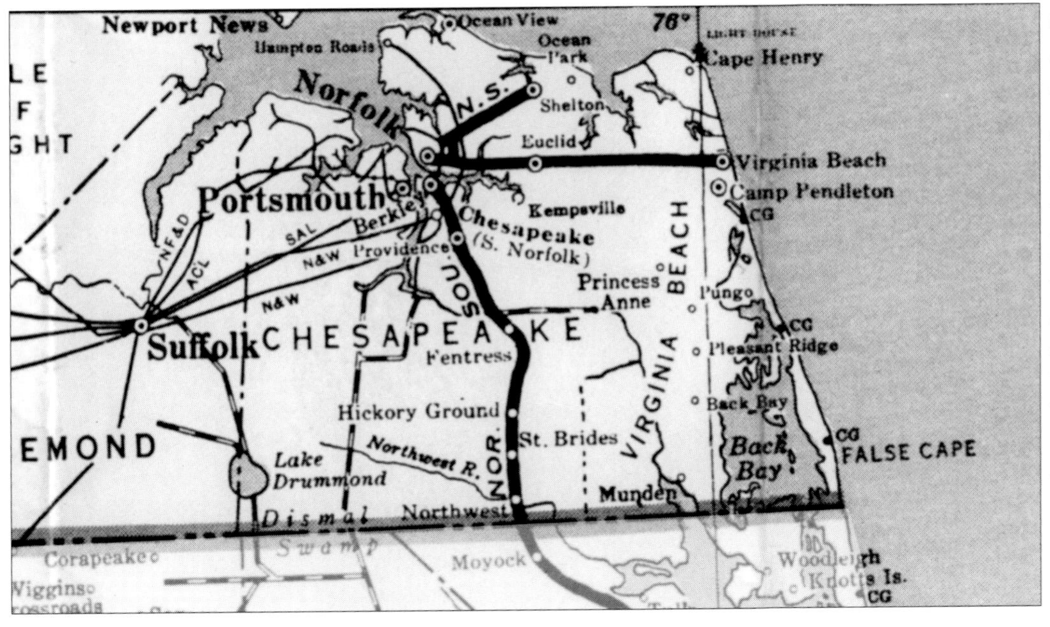

Beach to Cape Henry. In 1904 the NS purchased the Chesapeake Transit Company and now operated both electric routes from Norfolk to the beaches.

Since the NS now owned both routes to the beach, it joined the two lines at Norfolk through construction of nearly two miles of electrified trackage and created a loop line from Norfolk to Virginia Beach. The NS electric division was essentially a suburban passenger line used by those commuting to work year-round and tourists headed to the beach during the summer months. Passenger service began to wane in 1922 with the construction of the paved Virginia Beach Boulevard between Norfolk and the beaches. In 1935 gasoline powered motor cars replaced the electric traction equipment, and in 1948 passenger service was discontinued on the lines.

The Southern Railway acquired the NS in 1974 and merged the railroad into its subsidiary, the Carolina and Northwestern Railway, but did not change the NS name at that time. The name change occurred in 1982 when the merged company created by the merger of the Southern and N&W was named the Norfolk Southern Corporation.

In 1912 the new Norfolk Terminal Station was opened to serve the passenger trains of the Norfolk and Western, Virginian and Norfolk Southern. Initially the electric trains of the Norfolk Southern did not operate into the station and continued to stop at City Hall Avenue at the Monticello Arcade until 1919 when overhead wires were installed into the station for trolley operation. Norfolk Southern D-4 class 4-6-0 No. 132 is departing the Norfolk Terminal Station with Train No. 1 in 1938. The train has its regular consist of a RPO-baggage car, Express car and two coaches. (Richard E. Prince Photo/William E. Griffin, Jr. Collection)

Until 1940 all freight trains over the Norfolk Southern were powered by the railroad's fleet of impressive 2-8-0 locomotives, which remained in service until the end of steam. However, with WW II looming, the NS decided that it needed a new type of locomotive to pull the heavy war materiel and still meet bridge restrictions on its main line. In 1939 the railroad ordered five light 2-8-4 locomotives from Baldwin. These locomotives, numbered 600-604, were assigned to through freight service between Carolina Junction and Charlotte and improved both the tonnage and speed previously achieved by the Consolidations. No. 601 is shown passing the cinder pit that the Carolina Junction coaling station in 1948. These locomotives had a short career on the Norfolk Southern: all were retired in 1950 and eventually ended up working on Mexican railroads. (H. Reid Photo/William E. Griffin, Jr. Collection)

The Norfolk Southern began dieselization in 1947 when it purchased three Baldwin DS4-4-660's numbered 661-663. The railroad continued to purchase Baldwin power with two DS4-4-1000 locomotives (1001 and 1002) in 1946 and ten DRS6-4-1500 locomotives (1501-1510) in 1948. The lone non-Baldwin units purchased during that period were three GE 70-ton units (701-703) in 1948. The Norfolk Southern purchased its final Baldwin units between 1951 and 1955, seventeen AS416 locomotives (1601-1617). When the railroad received the first three of these in 1954 it retired all of its steam locomotives. Typical of the Baldwin units is DRS6-4-1500 No. 1506 at South Norfolk in 1955. (Bob Lorenz Photo/TLC Collection)

The Washington and Old Dominion Railway was a fascinating Virginia short line that began its long and complicated corporate history with great expectations, struggled through 120 years of mismanagement and missed opportunities leading to a series of bankruptcies and corporate reorganizations, and ended with a contentious demise. One fascinating aspect of the W&OD is not what it was, but what it might have been.

The W&OD's story began in 1847 when a group of Alexandria businessmen obtained a charter from the General Assembly to construct the Alexandria and Harper's Ferry Railroad, intended to capture some of the business that was moving from the west to Baltimore. No railroad was built under that charter and in 1853 the legislature approved a change in the company's name to the Alexandria, Loudoun & Hampshire Railroad and a change in route that would take the railroad west to Leesburg in Loudoun County, across the Blue Ridge Mountains, and into the coal fields of western Virginia. Construction began in 1855 and had been completed to Leesburg prior to the start of the War Between the States. That portion of the line west of Vienna was destroyed early in the war. The line east of Vienna was of strategic importance due to its proximity to Washington and it was seized by the union army and operated by the U. S. Military Railroad for the rest of the war.

The railroad was restored to its owners at the conclusion of the war and the line was reopened to Leesburg in 1867. New construction extended the line to Clark's Gap and in 1870 the company was again reorganized as the Washington & Ohio Railroad. The railroad attempted to press on with the westward expansion but the expense of construction resulted in bankruptcy and two reorganizations. It was reorganized as the Washington & Western Railroad in 1882 and as the Washington, Ohio & Western Railroad the following year. The railroad's name was a reflection of its owners aspirations – not a description of its actual right-of-way. The WO&W's tracks did not extend into Washington and they would never reach the Ohio River. The eastern end of the railroad was located in Alexandria, where it connected with the Orange & Alexandria Railroad. The western end of the line was at Round Hill, in western Loudoun County.

In 1886, the WO&W was leased by the Richmond & Danville Railroad, and was operated as a branch line of that railroad. The R&D was included in the Southern Railway on its creation in 1894. In 1900, the Southern extended the tracks of the WO&W to Snickersville and ran passenger trains to bring city folks to the boarding houses and summer hotels of the popular mountain resort located in that area. Snicksville would later assume the more socially appealing name of Bluemont. The entire line of the WO&W came to be known as the Bluemont Branch of the Southern Railway. From 1900 until about 1912, steam powered passenger trains were operated by the Southern Railway out of Union Station in Washington to Alexandria Junction (north of the current Old Town Alexandria), where they switched to the Bluemont

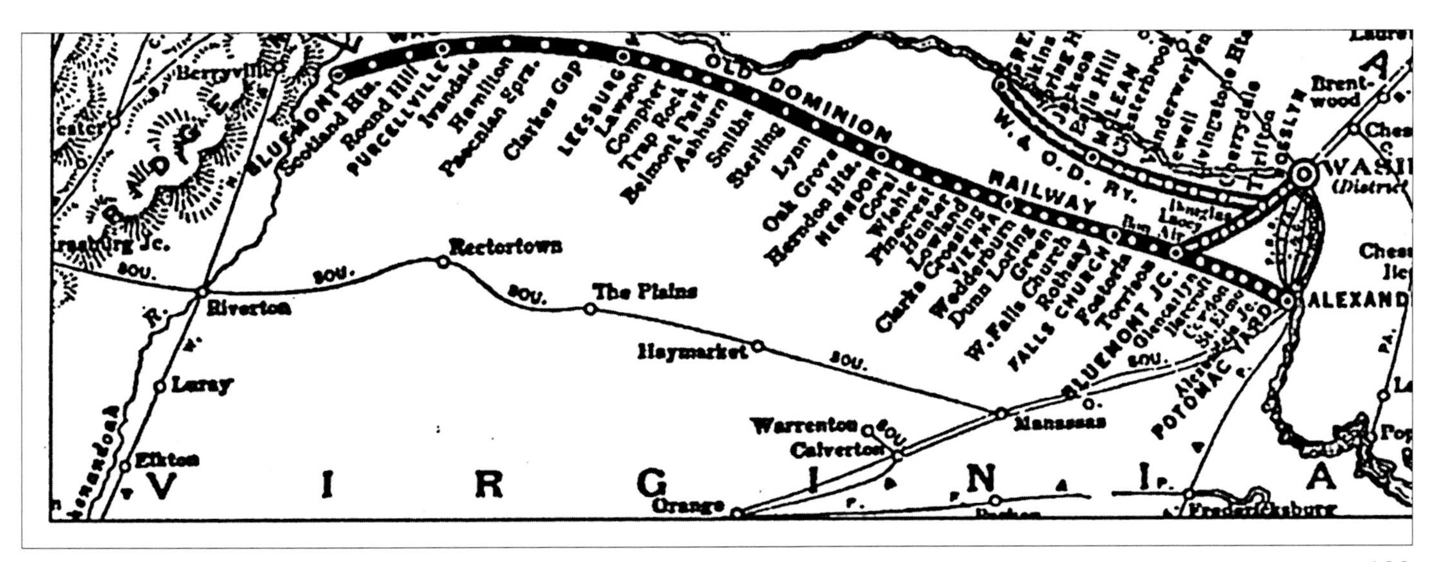

The Great Falls and Old Dominion Railroad was chartered to build an interurban trolley line from Georgetown to a recreational area that had been built at the Great Falls of the Potomac River. After crossing the Potomac River on the old Aqueduct Bridge, the line passed through Rosslyn to Cherrydale and then through farmland and countryside to reach Great Falls. Here is GF&OD trolley car No. 8 passing Pimmit Run in 1908. The wooden coach was built by Jackson & Sharp in 1906 and seated 42 passengers. This car was demolished in a wreck with car No. 15 at Vanderwerken on October 3, 1912 and was retired. (TLC Collection)

The W&OD Railroad was chartered in 1911 to acquire the Great Falls & Old Dominion and to lease the Washington, Ohio & Western Railroad from the Southern Railway. The GF&OD became the Great Falls Division and the WO&W became the Bluemont Divsion of the new W&OD Railroad. The W&OD then electrified all of the Bluemont Division to become a complete interurban electrical trolley system. The W&OD operated both passenger and freight with its electrified lines. This is a view of freight electric motor No. 26 with a freight train at Leesburg on September 8, 1919. The motor was wooden construction and was built by the W&OD in its Rosslyn shops in 1919 and was retired in 1944. (TLC Collection)

Branch for the trip to the mountain resorts.

During this period another railroad was being formed in Northern Virginia that would become a part of the W&OD. John R. McLean, the publisher of the Washington Post, and West Virginia Senator Stephen B. Elkins, purchased a large tract of land in Fairfax County adjacent to the Great Falls of the Potomac River where they constructed an amusement park and recreation area. In 1900 they obtained a charter for the Great Falls and Old Dominion Railroad, an interurban line that would operate electric trolleys to transport passengers from a station at Georgetown to their recreational area at Great Falls. The line was opened to Cherrydale in Arlington County in 1904 and to Great Falls in 1906. The line crossed the Potomac River on the old Aqueduct Bridge, passed through Rosslyn to Cherrydale and then through farmland and countryside to reach Great Falls.

The line to Great Falls was an initial success and its owners decided to expand their operation. In 1911, they obtained a charter for a new company – the Washington and Old Dominion Railway – to operate the GF&OD and to acquire the Southern Railway's lease of the WO&W. In 1912, the W&OD leased all of the WO&W (the Bluemont Branch) from the Southern Railway with the exception of a short segment of the line between Potomac Yard and old Alexandria Junction. The Southern then leased this section of track to the W&OD to enable it to reach the east side of Potomac Yard crossing the yard on a newly constructed trestle. The GF&OD became the Great Falls Division of the W&OD, and the WO&W became the Bluemont Division of the W&OD. A double track connnecting line was built between Bluemont Junction on the WO&W and Thrifton Junction on the GF&OD to join the railroad's two operating divisions.

Over the next four years, the W&OD electrified all of the Bluemont Division. Now the entire W&OD was an interurban electrical trolley system that operated trains for both freight and passengers. The new railroad had some issues. There had never been any high volume, high revenue freight traffic on the Bluemont Division. It was unlikely that the road would be able to attract any valuable freight business. There was also a glaring omission in its passenger service in that neither of the W&OD's lines had access to Union Station in Washington. The railroad's Washington passenger station was located at Rosslyn on the western bank of the Potomac River in Virginia across from Georgetown. In 1923 the W&OD gave up completely on the possibility of operating passenger service in Washington when it ceased its service from Georgetown.

The W&OD operated passenger service over the Bluemont Divison between Bluemont (until 1939 then Purcellville) and Alexandria. Here we see the "The Bluemont Local" at the Bluemont station on September 5, 1937. The W&OD owned steel and wood cars Nos. 42-44 that were built by the Southern Car Company in 1912. They were considered heavy interurban type cars and seated 38 passengers. (TLC Collection)

The W&OD was an early victim of the Great Depression of the 1930's. By 1932 it was bankrupt and being operated by a receiver. To cut costs, the receiver abandoned operations on the Great Falls Division between Thrifton Junction and Great Falls in 1934. When the road came out of receivership in 1936, it was reorganized again as the Washington and Old Domininon Railroad. The new railroad began operation with the Bluemont Division, the connecting line and what remained of the Great Falls Division between Rosslyn and Thrifton. In 1935, Fairfax and Arlington counties obtained the W&OD's right-of-way west of Thrifton Junction in a settlement with the railroad for outstanding taxes. Tracks on the western end of the Bluemont Division were removed in 1939 between Bluemont and Purcellville. East of Purcellville, stations were closed at West Falls Church, Sterling and Paeonian Springs. Passenger service was discontinued on the entire railroad in 1941.

The W&OD's operation of electric locomotives came to an end during the 1940's. The obsolete and wornout trolleys were replaced by diesel and gas-electric powered engines. The first diesels acquired by the W&OD were low horsepower GE 44-ton and Whitcomb 70-ton locomotives that helped the railroad with the boom in traffic that it enjoyed during the Second World War. When the federal government forced the W&OD to reinstate passenger service during the war it scrambled to find equipment to replace the cars that had been scrapped when it discontinued the service in 1941. It was able to purchase a diesel-electric powered train (motorcar and trailer car) from the Pennsylvania Railroad. The railroad also innovated by having a diesel locomotive pull a gas-electric that could not operate under its own power. Passenger and mail service were discontinued over the W&OD in 1951.

The W&OD changed owners for the last time in 1956 when it was sold to the Chesapeake and Ohio Railway. The C&O did not change the railroad's name and operated the W&OD as a wholly owned subsidiary. At that time there was a political contest between the states of Virginia and Maryland to locate a new PEPCO coal fired power plant on their side of the Potomac River. The site that was being considered for the plant in Virginia was along the line of W&OD. The C&O was gambling that Virginia would prevail and that it would then be able to handle the shipments of coal to the new facility. Unfortunately for the C&O, PEPCO decided to locate the new plant in Maryland.

The C&O's purchase of the W&OD was saved from being a complete failure when the federal government selected a site near Sterling for the construction of the new Dulles International Airport. The W&OD was in a position to move construction materials for new airport and the C&O upgraded the railroad between Potomac Yard and Sterling with new rails, ties and bridges to accommodate heavier loads. The upgraded bridges allowed the W&OD to replace its 44-ton and 70-ton locomotives with more powerful diesels.

However, by the 1960's it was becoming increasing clear – especially to the C&O – that the real value of the W&OD was in its right-of-way, not in the revenues that could be generated by operating a railroad. In 1962, the C&O turned a nice profit by abandoning and then selling to the state the 2.9 miles of line between Rosslyn and Thrifton to make way for the construction of Interstate 66. In 1965, the C&O reached an agreement with the state to sell the entire W&OD if approval for abandonment of the line could be obtained from the Interstate Commerce Commission. The C&O filed an application to abandon the line and when the ICC recommended abandonment it set off a contentious three year battle at the ICC and in the courts. Certain shippers opposed abandonment as did the Washington Metropolitan Area Transit Authority, which wanted a study to determine rapid transit uses for the line. In the end the railroad was allowed to abandon its line and the last operations occurred on August 27, 1968.

One can only wonder what might have happened with the W&OD if it had successfully extended its line to West Virginia, or if the PEPCO plant had located on its line, or if the right-of-way had been utilized as a rapid transit route in Northern Virginia. But those opportunities were missed and while the memories remain the railroad only exists today as a group of popular bike and hiking trails that utilize its former right-of-way.

Freight electric motor No. 50 was built by Baldwin-Westinghouse in 1920. It is shown in freight service on the W&OD at Rosslyn in May of 1939. In 1947, the W&OD sold the motor to the Cedar Rapids & Iowa City Railroad. (TLC Collection)

To provide passenger service during the Second World War the W&OD leased and later purchased a diesel-electric powered train (motorcar and trailer) from the Pennsylvania Railroad in 1943. The train was built by Budd in 1932, and is shown here at the Rosslyn yard in June of 1943. (TLC Collection)

When required to reinstate passenger service during the war the W&OD also innovated by having its diesel locomotives pull the gas-electrics that could not operate under their own power and were used as trailer coaches. Here diesel No. 49 is attached to interurban coach No. 46 at Rosslyn for the afternoon run to Purcellville in August of 1950. Diesel No. 49 was a class BB 380-horsepower unit built by GE in 1942. (TLC Collection)

Incorporated March 4, 1896, as the Southeastern and Atlantic Railroad Company, in 1898 the name was changed to the Norfolk and Portsmouth Belt Line Railroad Company. Its purpose was constructing, maintaining and operating a standard-gauge railroad around the cities of Berkley and Portsmouth, Virginia, and connecting the eight railroad lines entering the Hampton Roads territory. The N&PBL was controlled by the railroads it connected: Atlantic Coast Line, Atlantic and Danville, Chesapeake and Ohio, Norfolk and Western, Seaboard Air Line, Southern, Norfolk and Southern (Norfolk Southern RR) and the New York, Pennsylvania & Norfolk (PRR). A&D's ownership ceased in 1908 and Virginian was added in 1909 when it was completed to Sewalls Point.

N&PBL originally owned 5.7 miles of main line tracks from Port Norfolk to Berkley (3.3 miles were doubled tracked), and a 6-mile branch from Berkley to Burrell, with over 22 miles of yard tracks and sidings. It operated on 1.8 miles of main track owned by A&D (the former Portsmouth branch) per an agreement with the Southern Railway, the lessee of the A&D. The N&PBL interchanged with the N&W and N&S (Norfolk Southern after 1911) at Berkley. Connection with the PRR's NYP&N RR was made at Port Norfolk. From car float slips located on the south shore of the Elizabeth River, PRR barged its freight traffic to and from Cape Charles on the Eastern Shore when it built its new Little Creek terminal. The N&PBL then crossed the tracks of the ACL and interchanged with both ACL and Southern just south of their terminals at Pinners Point. The N&PBL's shops and yard were located just north of High Street in Portsmouth, where SAL tracks were crossed and connection made with that road south of SAL's shops. The Virginian connected with the N&PBL via Norfolk Southern tracks between Berkley and Carolina Junction. C&O's connection with N&PBL was via a car float between Port Norfolk and C&O's Brooke Avenue yard in Norfolk.

During the WWI N&PBL acquired ten miles of trackage rights over the Virginian from Carolina Junction to Boush Junction. Two

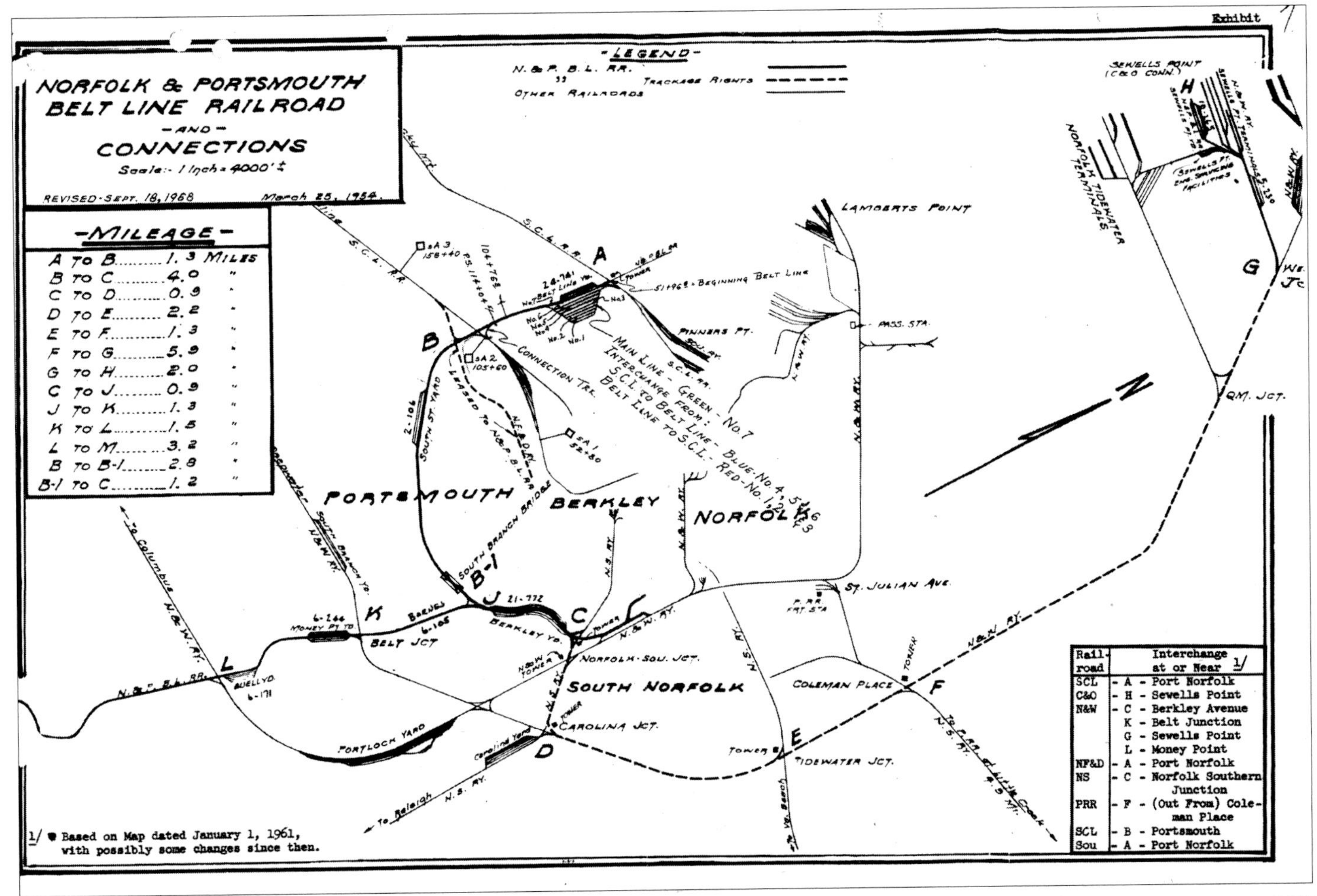

miles of new N&PBL trackage were then constructed between Bouch Junction to a new terminal near Sewells Point. Additional N&PBL trackage was then built to Tidewater Terminal. Today the N&PBL owns 36 miles of track and has trackage rights over 27 miles of track.

During the steam era, the N&PBL owned a fleet of 0-6-0 and 2-8-0 locomotives. Several were built new by Baldwin, and others were acquired second hand from the PRR. N&PBL also acquired 4-8-0s and 2-8-0s from N&W and 0-6-0s from ACL, SAL and RF&P. A group of US Army 0-6-0's that had been operated as 2-6-0's on the Midland Terminal Railway were converted back to 0-6-0's by the N&PBL. Steam operations ended in 1956 with the delivery of fifteen SW-1200 EMD diesel switchers (Nos. 101-115). They were quite colorfully painted in a EMD-inspired maroon, red and yellow scheme. They were replaced, beginning in 1988, by second hand EMD SW1500's and MP15DC's from the Southern Railway that were painted black with minimal lettering to identify them as N&PBL engines. In 2003, several ex-Conrail GP15's (also in black paint with white lettering) began to replace some of the ex-Southern switchers.

As the N&PBL's original eight owners merged, ownership changed, beginning with VGN and N&W in 1959, and then ACL and SAL in 1967. With each merger came consolidation of facilities and operational changes. For example, one of the ICC's conditions for the approval of the ACL/SAL merger was the Southern's cancellation of its lease to operate over the ACL from Selma, N. C. to Pinners Point. Southern would access Hampton Roads over the Norfolk Southern. Also, when Norfolk Southern closed its Carolina Yard, its locomotive servicing was moved to N&PBL shops in Portsmouth. Mergers also resulted in major traffic and revenue losses for the N&PBL. Its Portsmouth Yard was closed in 1955 and the Pinners Point rail and shipping ceased in 1962. Penn Central (former Pennsylvania Railroad) ownership in N&PBL ended with the creation of Conrail in 1976, leaving SCL, N&W, Southern and Chessie System as owners. After the merger of the SCL and Chessie to create CSX, and N&W and Southern to create Norfolk Southern (the new NS Corporation) ownership of N&PBL was reduced to two. Today, CSX owns forty-three percent and Norfolk Southern fifty-seven percent of the N&PBL. The N&PBL interchanges with those two roads and with the Bay Coast Railroad and the Chesapeake and Albemarle Railroad short lines. Unlike many of the Virginia short lines that now are abandoned, the N&PBL continues to be the connecting link for rail commerce in Hampton Roads from Sewells Point to Portsmouth Marine Terminal.

During the 60 year period that the N&PBL operated steam locomotives its roster contained a fleet of more than 50 locomotives. The roster primarily included 0-6-0 and 2-8-0 type locomotives and the majority of its locomotives were purchased second hand from other railroads. N&PBL 2-8-0 No. 41, shown here at Tidewater Junction on February 28, 1948 was a former Pennsylvania Railroad locomotive. (William B. Gwaltney Photo/TLC Collection)

The Atlantic and Danville Railway served Southside Virginia extending westward for 205 miles from the Portsmouth and Norfolk area to Danville.

It was originally chartered in 1882 as a narrow gauge railroad. A 50-mile line of three-foot gauge track was completed from Claremont on the James River to Belfield (now Emporia) in 1885, financed by subscriptions of the counties through which the line would pass. When construction of the line reached Belfield, the ambitions of its builders expanded and the company was reincorporated in 1886 with authority to move the principal deep water terminal to the Norfolk area and then to construct a standard gauge railroad from Portsmouth west to Danville by way of a connection with the narrow gauge line near Belfield at James River Junction. The narrow gauge line was never rebuilt to standard gauge and was thereafter relegated to branch line status.

Construction of the standard gauge line was financed by a large investment of British capitalists who desired to use the railroad to ship cotton to the port of Norfolk, and thence to England. However, the expense of constructing the standard gauge line quickly drove the company into bankruptcy and receivership. This led to a reorganization in 1894 and the railroad came under control of its English investors.

In 1899, the A&D's owners in England leased the entire railroad to the Southern Railway for a period of fifty years. The Southern had achieved an entrance into the port of Norfolk in 1896 by leasing the North Carolina Railroad and entering into a trackage rights arrangement with the Atlantic Coast Line Railroad. This allowed the Southern to extend its operations from Charlotte, North Carolina to Pinners Point, Virginia. However, the Southern's situation at Norfolk was somewhat precarious. While the railroad had made substantial expenditures to build its Pinners Point facilities, it was permanently dependent on the lease of the North Carolina Railroad and ACL trackage rights to reach them. By leasing the A&D, the Southern was able to protect its investment at Pinners Point with another route that would be separate and independent of the North Carolina Railroad lease and the ACL trackage rights agreement.

Because the Southern preferred to use its own terminal and piers at Pinners Point and concentrated all of its Norfolk traffic at that location, after beginning operation under the lease, they abandoned the A&D's terminal at West Norfolk and routed all freight traffic through Pinners Point. To reach Pinners Point from the A&D, the Southern obtained trackage rights over the ACL from Boone to Pinners Point Junction. The Southern also favored operating into the Norfolk area via its trackage rights over the ACL's route from Selma, North Carolina.

During the period of its lease, the Southern gradually reduced the through freight service over the A&D and it was operated as just another Southern branch line. Freight service consisted of one local freight train in each direction, daily-except-Sunday, between Pinners Point and Lawrenceville and between Lawrenceville and Danville. The typical freight transit time between Pinners Point and Danville was two days. The Southern also operated a switcher between Pinners Point, West Norfolk and Suffolk on week days.

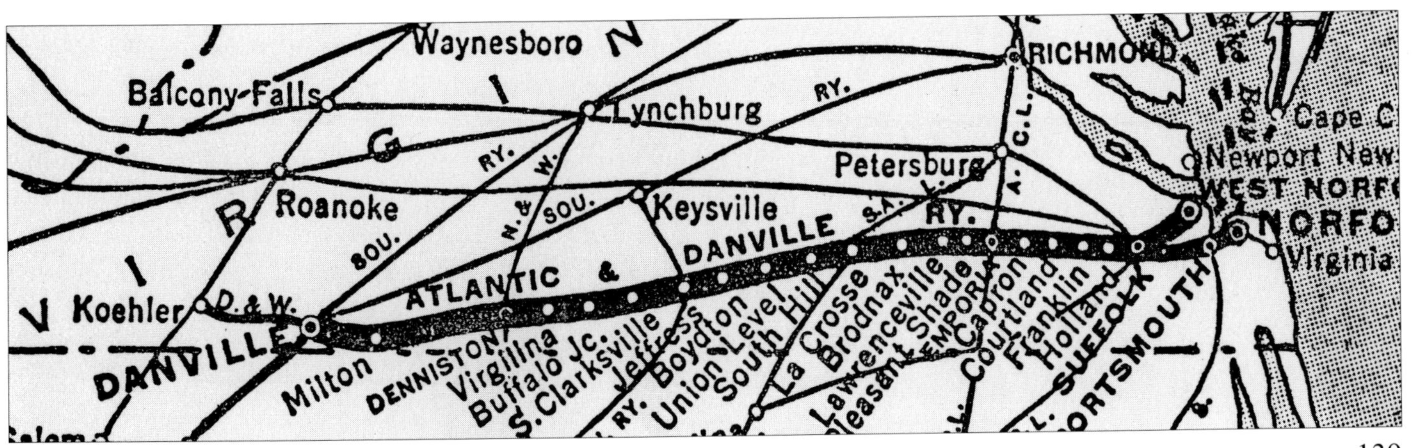

The A&D was originally built as a narrow gauge line between Claremont and Emporia. When the railroad was reorganized in 1886 as a standard gauge line between Norfolk and Danville, the line to Claremont became a narrow gauge branch line until abandoned in 1932. Service over the branch consisted of a daily-except-Sunday mixed train (Nos. 103 and 104) between Claremont and Emporia. Here we see Train No. 104 with 4-6-0 No. N6 arriving in Claremont Wharf in the summer of 1910. The train departed Emporia at 7 a.m. and reached Claremont around noon with scheduled stops at James River Junction, Gary, Yale, Homeville, Waverly and Spring Grove. The A&D line between James River Junction (where the Claremont Branch joined the Norfolk to Danville main line) and Emporia was dual gauge trackage to permit the operation of both narrow and standard guage trains. (Shelby F Lowe Collection)

During the lease the Southern scheduled two daily through passenger trains each way between Norfolk and Danville, a daily-except-Sunday local between Lawrenceville and Danville and several branch line mixed trains. Train Nos. 1 and 2 departed in the early morning for their 7-hour daily Norfolk-Danville runs until finally discontinued in 1940. Train Nos. 3 and 4 operated daily between Norfolk and Danville on a night schedule. They offered Pullman drawing-room sleeping car service between Norfolk and Charlotte, North Carolina, connecting with the Southern main line trains at Danville. Passengers to and from Norfolk and were boarded and detrained at the Pinners Point depot with ferry service across the Elizabeth River to the Southern's wharf in Norfolk at the foot of Jackson Street. In the final years of passenger service, buses provided the transportation between Pinners Point and Norfolk.

In 1932 the Southern strengthened eight bridges on the A&D to permit operation of 2-8-0 type locomotives in freight service. Since these locomotives were permitted to operate double-headed and could handle all of the tonnage routed over the A&D line, the Southern found no justification for strengthening the A&D bridges for the operation of Mikado type locomotives. Hence, the K and Ks class 2-8-0's were the heaviest steam locomotives to operate over the A&D. By the 1930's most passenger runs were assigned to light Pacifics of the Ps, Ps-1 and Ps-2 classes. These locomotives were painted in the distinctive green and gold paint scheme fostered by Southern's President Fairfax Harrison.

During the Great Depression freight traffic was further reduced over the A&D route, and the Southern abandoned service on all of the former A&D branch lines. The narrow gauge branch line between Emporia and Claremont was the first line to be abandoned in 1932. By the 1940's the Southern had come to view its lease of the A&D as both unprofitable and unnecessary. There were yearly deficits in the local operation over the A&D and the Southern had no intention of diverting the through traffic from the Selma route. In 1944 the Southern formally advised the British owners of the A&D that it would not seek a renewal of the lease.

Southern's decision not to renew the lease led to a five-year legal battle between the Southern and the A&D's British owners. The most difficult issue to be resolved involved the Southern's obligations concerning restoration of the A&D property upon termination of the lease. Among other things the A&D demanded that the Southern restore the terminal at West Norfolk and locomotive shops at Lawrenceville. After A&D won the first round when the Norfolk County Circuit Court found in its favor, the two companies resumed negotiations and eventually reached a settlement agreement which led to the A&D's second period of independent operation beginning on August 1, 1949.

Under the settlement, the A&D acquired terminal facilities at Pinners Point and trackage rights over the ACL from Boone to Pinners Point Junction to reach both Pinners Point and interchange with the Norfolk and Portsmouth Belt Line. The Southern agreed to act as a friendly connection of the A&D and to participate with it in numerous through routes and joint rates. It also agreed to perform maintenance work for the A&D and to return a certain number of rolling stock, other than locomotives and floating equipment. The Southern also reached a cash settlement with A&D, which the new railroad used to purchase a fleet of new Alco RS-2 diesel locomotives. One RS-3 was acquired in 1951 and two RS-36s arrived during what would be the final days of the railroad's existence. The A&D used these new diesels to create a new daily overnight through freight service in each direction between Norfolk and Danville and shorten the transit time over the A&D from two days to less than nine hours.

For several years the A&D operated successfully. Then two unfortunate train wrecks in 1952 aggravated the A&D's growing problems of low revenues and increased expenses for equipment and facilities rental. The company's condition continued to worsen as it lacked funds to maintain its property and locomotives. By 1957, the A&D was required to negotiate loans each year to meet the interest payments on its bonds and satisfy the outstanding debt on equipment and obligations. In 1960 the A&D filed for bankruptcy and its attempt for independent operation came to an end in 1962 when the company's assets were purchased by the Norfolk and Western Railway. The property was renamed the Norfolk, Franklin and Danville Railway and was operated as a wholly owned subsidiary of the N&W. A large portion of the NF&D was abandoned after the N&W/Southern merger and creation of the Norfolk Southern Corporation in 1982. The railroad finally lost its separate corporate identity when it was absorbed into the N&W in December 1983 and was operated as the Franklin District of the N&W's Norfolk Division.

Train Nos. 1 and 2 were operated by the SRR on a daily 7-hour schedule between Norfolk and Danville until the train were discontinued in 1940. Train Nos. 3 and 4 continued to operate until the end of the lease in 1949. Ps class 4-6-2 No. 1227 pulls Train No. 1 away from Boydton in May of 1937 on its scheduled run to Danville. Operated on local schedule, No. 1 was scheduled to depart Boydton at 1:30 p.m. and arrived in Danville at 4:00 p.m. after making scheduled stops at South Clarksville, Buffalo Junction, Virgilina, Denniston, Semora, Milton and Blanche.(Thomas G. Moore photo/William E. Griffin, Jr. Collection)

Freight service over the A&D during the period of the SRR lease consisted of one local freight train in each direction daily-except-Sunday between Danville and Lawrenceville and between Lawrenceville and Pinners Point. In a typical view of these trains SRR Ks class 2-8-0 No. 682 is stopping at Boydton with the westbound local in 1949. The first car behind the locomotive is SU-class 36-foot boxcar No. 524 that was used for a number of years as the express car over the A&D. (Flourney Photo/Virginia State Library)

When the SRR did not renew its lease of the A&D, the new railroad knew that it would have to compete with its former lessee for the business between Norfolk and Danville. The A&D's strategy was to establish a new daily overnight service (Trains Nos. 85/86) that would shorten the through freight transit time from two days to less than nine hours. On a slower schedule, the A&D also operated Trains 69/70 between Norfolk and Danville daily-except-Sunday. On March 10, 1959, eastbound Train No. 70 with RS-2 No. 101 meets its westbound counterpart No. 70 with RS-2 No. 103 at Franklin. (Mallory Hope Ferrell Photo)

The Danville and Western Railway was a 75-mile short line that operated between Danville and Stuart, Virginia with a branch line to Leaksville (Eden), North Carolina. It was incorporated for the purpose of acquiring and operating the Danville and New River Railroad.

The Danville and New River Railroad had been granted a charter by the Virginia General Assembly in 1873 for the purpose of building a narrow gauge railroad from Danville via Martinsville to some point in Montgomery County on the Atlantic, Mississippi & Ohio Railroad (a predecessor of the Norfolk and Western Railway). Its founders had intended that the railroad would be a westward connection for the textile and tobacco industries of Danville. Work did not begin on the line for almost a decade until the railroad reached an agreement with Patrick County to assist in financing its construction. In December of 1879, crews began laying the 3-foot narrow gauge tracks on the 43-mile segment from Danville to Martinsville. The line was completed to Martinsville in 1881 and another 32-mile segment reached the Patrick County Courthouse (Stuart) in 1884.

As the construction of the Danville and New River progressed, the railroad obtained a charter from the state of North Carolina to build branch lines twenty miles in length from any point on the line in Virginia into North Carolina. In 1881 construction began of the Danville, Mocksville & Southwestern Railroad (a 7-mile 3-foot gauge branch line) from Danville to Leaksville, North Carolina. The line was opened in 1882 and went bankrupt in 1885. The Danville and New River also went bankrupt and was placed in the hands of a receiver in 1887.

With both of these lines being operated by a receiver, a new company - the Danville and Western Railway - was chartered in 1891 to acquire and operate the bankrupt properties. It took over operation of the Danville & New River in 1891 and acquired in Danville, Mocksville & Southwestern in 1899. The reorganization plan that created the Danville and Western was proposed and guaranteed by the Richmond and Danville Railroad (the predecessor company of the Southern Railway). The Richmond and Danville saw these railroads as a way to block the Baltimore and Ohio Railroad's Shenandoah Valley line from extending into the state of North Carolina. The Danville and Western would be wholly owned but separately operated by the Richmond and Danville and its successor, the Southern Railway, until 1951.

Between 1900-1903, the entire Danville and Western was changed from 3-foot to standard gauge. By 1916, the Danville and Western was operating 77 miles of main line track and 12 miles of yard track. It was owned 9 steam locomotives, 122 freight cars and 14 passenger cars. The railroad was never extended and the "Dick and Willie", as it was locally known, was operated as a wholly owned short line of the Southern Railway until 1951, when it became the Martinsville Division of the Southern Railway's Carolina and Northwestern Railway.

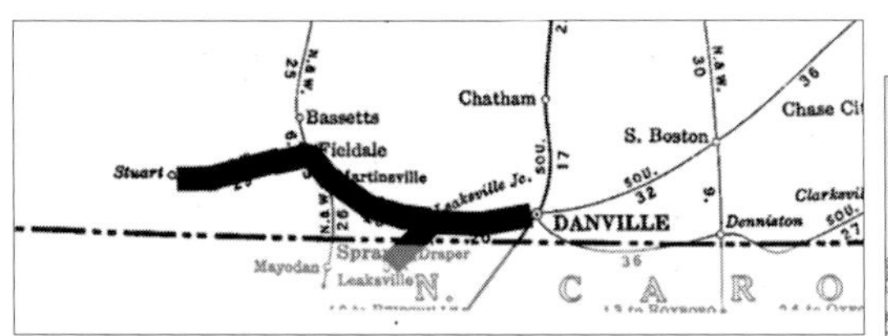

The Danville and Western Railway - fondly called the "Dick and Willie" or the "Delay and Wait" - operated at leisurely pace along its 75-mile route on the Virginia and North Carolina border between Danville and Stuart, Virginia. During the steam era the railroad operated its trains with a roster of seven 4-6-0's and three 2-8-0's locomotives. Typical of its motive power was 4-6-0 No. 22 that was built new for the railroad in 1907. The handsome locomotive is resting between assignments at Danville on May 19, 1940. (C. W. Whitbeck Photo/TLC Collection)

The Virginia Central Railway - not to be confused with the Chesapeake and Ohio Railway's predecessor railroad of the same name - traced its corporate beginning to1853 when the Fredericksburg and Gordonsville Railroad was authorized by the Virginia General Assembly. At the initial stockholders meeting they voted to build west to Orange Court House rather than southwest to Gordonsville. However, little work was done to construct the line until after the War Between the States. With only 18 miles line graded between Fredericksburg and Parkers, the stockholders forced a foreclosure of the railroad in 1871.

A new corporation known as the Fredericksburg, Orange & Charlottesville, backed by northern investors, purchased the foreclosed line. However, this corporation laid only 18 miles of track on the previously graded line and it was also sold in foreclosure in 1873. In 1876 the railroad was again reorganized and its name changed to the Potomac, Fredericksburg and Potomac Railroad. The new owners converted the whole railroad to narrow gauge and completed the line from Parkers to Orange in 1877. The Potomac, Fredericksburg and Potomac was operated as a 38-mile narrow gauge line until it also failed and sold in foreclosure in 1925. The line was again reorganized as the Orange & Fredericksburg Railroad but its owners were unable to attract investors to operate the line. Obviously, potential investors had noticed the railroad's history of corporate failures.

Yet one brave investor stepped forward. Langbourne Williams, a Richmond banker who had been a president of the Seaboard Air Line Railroad, purchased the line in 1926. He rebuilt the railroad to standard gauge and changed its name to the Virginia Central Railway. He also had a plan for the line. Williams intended to extend the railroad east of Fredericksburg along the south bank of the Rappahannock River to a new port that would be built at its mouth near the Chesapeake Bay. The Great Depression intervened and the eastern extension was never started. The line from Fredericksburg to Orange was operated with group of 2-8-0 steam locomotives purchased from the Western Maryland, C&O and N&W. Beginning in 1927 passenger service was provided by a Brill gas-electric railcar, the M100, purchased from the Santa Fe Railroad.

In 1938 the entire line of the Virginia Central was abandoned except for one mile of main line and a mile and a quarter of side track, all within the city limits of Fredericksburg. The Virginia Central's primary revenues were derived from its interchange of traffic with the RF&P for a group of industrial customers that were located in West Fredericksburg. The steam locmotives were replaced by a succession of gas-electric industrial locomotives suitable for such service. In 1967 the Williams family transferred ownership of the little railroad to Fredericksburg. However, the deteriorating condition of the railroad and its equipment made it difficult for the city to turn a profit and from 1975 to 1978, the railroad was owned by Railvest, a boxcar investment firm. Railvest also proved to be a failure and in 1978 the railroad ceased operations.

VC 2-8-0 No. 901 (ex C&O 901) is set to depart Fredericksburg with a freight train on January 30, 1932. It is unfortunate that the entire railroad with the exception of the mile of industrial trackage was abandoned in 1938. There were very few photographers taking pictures of trains in the 1930s. As a result of the early demise of the railroad, photos such as this of the steam operations are extremely rare. (TLC Collection)

VIRGINIAN
VIRGINIAN
VIRGINIAN